Kidding Around the Gorge

Kidding Around the Gorge would not have been possible without the help from my family and friends, who are all eager and willing to join me on adventures through the Gorge. I also want to thank Jody Barringer who teamed with me to create the first Kidding Around the Gorge book.

A huge thank you to my husband Tim who spent many late nights putting this new version together. He is the computer/graphic/layout designer extraordinaire. Another big thank you to Karen Bullard, who helped me with photographs and inspiration. Maps were expertly created by Mike Schrankel. Big thanks to proofers and sounding boards Monique Pelletier-Anderson, Kass Bergstrom, Sue Davis, Mary Jane Heppe, Gretchen Newcomb and Liz Whitmore. Photographs were graciously given by Monique Pelletier-Anderson, Jody Barringer, Aaron Baumhackl, Connie Betts, Sherri Bradfield, Clint Bogard, Tony Bolstad, Kelly Brown, Karen Bullard, Lorraine Carlstrom, Cloud 9, Michelle Dearing, Robin Dickinson, Kevin Donald, Patty Gallagher, Kris Goodwillie, Susan Harkness, Hood River News (Dave Leder, Jim Semlor and Erik Steighner), Dave and Claire Howe, Jaco Klinkenburg, Kai Lai, Jenny Loughmiller, Susan Lucas, David and Mendy Maccabee, Peter Marbach, Maura Muhl, Tim Ortlieb, Dane Peterson, Eric Peterson, Terese Roeseler, Rena Russell, Peter Rysavy, Susan Shepherd, and Chris VanTilburg. Thank you!

Printed in Hood River, OR by Columbia Gorge Press.
ISBN: 0-9741861-0-4

Cover photo: Clark Hiking at Tom McCall Nature Preserve, photograph by Karen Bullard
Back cover photo: Swinging Happily, photograph by Robin Dickinson
Maps: Mike Schrankel
Please send us your feedback or any fun pictures of kids playing in the Gorge.
Kidding Around the Gorge
510 Highline Road
Hood River, OR 97031
ruthb@gorge.net

To my adventurers

Kai, Maya and Tim (and Jedi)

Thank you for exploring with me!

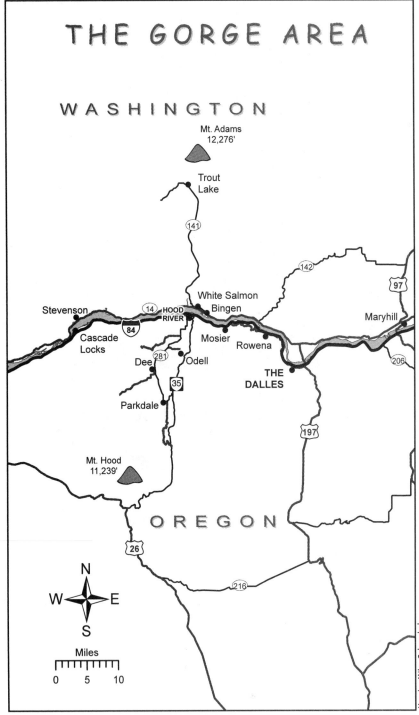

THE GORGE AREA

WASHINGTON

Mt. Adams
12,276'

Trout
Lake

141

142

97

White Salmon
Bingen

Stevenson

14 HOOD
RIVER

84

Maryhill

Cascade
Locks

Mosier

Rowena

206

Dee

281

Odell

THE
DALLES

35

Parkdale

197

Mt. Hood
11,239'

OREGON

26

216

N
W   E
S

Miles
0   5   10

Map by Mike Schrankel

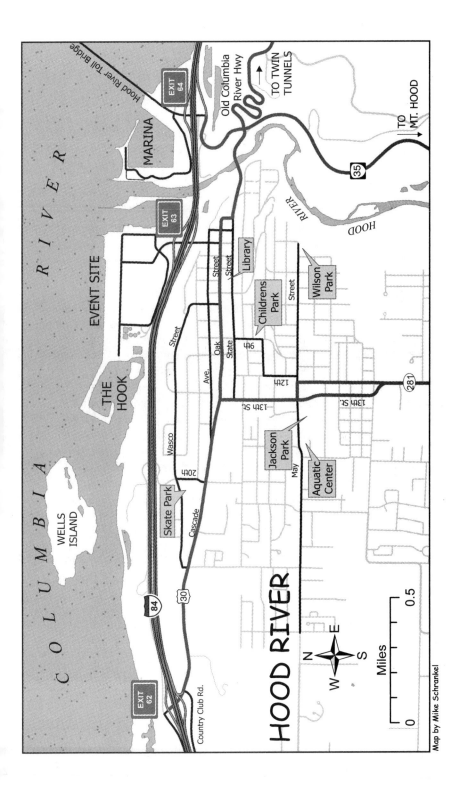

COLUMBIA R I V E R

WELLS ISLAND

Hood River Toll Bridge

EXIT 64

MARINA

EVENT SITE

THE HOOK

EXIT 63

Old Columbia River Hwy

TO TWIN TUNNELS

35

HOOD RIVER

TO MT. HOOD

Library

Childrens Park

Wilson Park

Street

Street

Street

Oak

State

9th

12th

281

13th St.

13th St.

Jackson Park

Aquatic Center

May

Ave.

Wasco

20th

Cascade

Skate Park

Street

30

84

EXIT 62

Country Club Rd.

HOOD RIVER

N
W   E
S

Miles

0   0.5

Map by Mike Schrankel

Introduction

I'm so glad you're holding the new and improved copy of Kidding Around the Gorge. This second edition gives you the inside scoop of places to go and things to do in the Columbia River Gorge with your kids. Because the Gorge is also a premier cycling area, we've added a new section on biking, a chapter on Winter Fun and many new places to visit and things to do. Since the first book published in 2003, the Gorge has changed. Another change is that our kids have gotten older, and we've included lots of activities for older children. Rain or shine, you'll find that the Gorge is full of opportunities for fun and adventure — whether you want to hike, ski, bike, throw rocks, go to a museum, take a class, pick fruit or eat ice cream. It's all here.

Not only is the Gorge a huge playground, but it's also a magical place to raise a family. It seems like there is always something going on. As you explore the area, you'll see why kids together with their parents and grandparents are smiling — not to mention very busy kidding around outside in the fresh air.

I've been kidding around the Gorge since my family settled in Hood River in 2001. When we moved here with two children, both under two, there was no road-map guiding us to kid-friendly places. Jody Barringer and I asked other parents where they liked to go and we kept exploring. We wrote the first Kidding Book to let other families know about the amazing adventures around us. We wrote the first book pretty quickly. This second edition adds another five years of exploration. We intentionally do not include a detailed and exhaustive list of things to do or places to go. Instead, we provide you with the best things for you and your family. When you're not sure what to do for the day or you have a few hours earmarked for exploration, open this book.

All activities listed are kid-tested. Places with a super smile next to them means that if you are here for only a short time, then these are the things that you don't want to miss.

I have not received any endorsements. What follows is my own opinion and ideas that I wanted to pass on to you.

Thanks for reading and Happy Kidding!

Table of Contents

How to Use This Book

This book divides into 18 chapters ranging from playing at playgrounds, to hiking and biking to picking fruit and winter fun. Each chapter includes a description of choice activities which are numbered for reference purposes. Altogether, you'll find more than 200 different places to go or do with your child or someone else's child.

Most activities include a "Getting There" section. That's to make sure you don't drive in circles, like I have numerous times. I've tried to write the directions as straightforward as possible. To be consistent, all directions start from Hood River. To supplement the directions, there are maps created by Mike Schrankel. These maps, located throughout the book, are general in nature and do not contain every single street. I encourage you to pick up a more detailed map of the Gorge at one of the visitor centers in town or to consult the Internet.

In Appendix B, the information is organized by location. That way, if you find yourself in The Dalles, Mosier, or any other town in the Gorge, you can look at Appendix B and get a bunch of ideas of where to go or what to do.

Smiley faces indicate the exceptional outings. Although everything listed in the book is worthwhile, the places with the super smile are the best of the best. If you have a limited time in the Gorge, make sure to go to the super smiles.

And lastly, I want to warn you that there is some repetition because not everything fits in a square peg or a round hole. For example, Lost Lake is an ideal place to hike, swim and fish so you'll find it mentioned in a number of chapters. I've tried to minimize the repetition, but sometimes ... well I don't want to repeat myself here. Just use the book, keep it in your purse or car and have fun in the Gorge.

Chapter 1

Monkeying Around the Playground

When your kids have turned your house into a playground by using the curtains as swings and the bed as a trampoline, you know it's time to head to a park. Rest assured, we have many fun parks for your children to let their wild energy gallop freely. Remember to bring sunscreen during the summer and hats in the winter.

Summer swinging at Wilson Park

Photo by Clint Bogard

Children's Park * Daubenspeck Park * Hood River Waterfront Park * Jackson Park * Sorosis Park * Toll Bridge Park * Wilson Park

☻Children's Park _____ 1

☞ **Location:** *Hood River, OR*

Built by the community of Hood River in just five days, the Children's Park is the town's most popular park and most social one. The wooden play structures include slides, tunnels, a large tic-tac-toe game, a sand area and lots of places to explore. There are usually plenty of friendly parents around and comfortable benches to sit down and enjoy the day. There's also a covered basketball court and a large grassy area for picnics and freeze

Blair swinging like a monkey.

Photo by Robin Dickinson

tag. Be warned that this park can be especially exposed to the hot summer sun so pack sun hats and check the slides on the playground -- the metal can be boiling to touch. With the numerous structures and play areas, children can get lost. Public restrooms, but locked in the winter.

🚶 **Getting There:** From downtown, go west on Oak St. Make a left at 9th St., drive up the hill a few blocks and turn left on Hazel St. *(541) 386-2383, www.ci.hood-river.or.us*

Daubenspeck Park _____ 2

☞ **Location:** *Bingen, WA*

This playground in Bingen (rhymes with "Engin") has colorful and challenging play structures, well-suited for the five to seven year olds. If you have a young adventurer, make sure to keep an eye on her as she may need a little help to reach the slides even if she doesn't think so. For the baseball player, remember to bring balls to try your swing at the baseball backstop. Public restrooms.

🚶 **Getting There:** From I-84 go north on Exit 64 and cross the Hood River Toll Bridge. On the Washington side, turn right onto Hwy. 14. Drive one mile and turn left on Willow St. You'll see the sign for "City Park". *City of Bingen, (509) 493-2122*

Hood River Waterfront Park _____3

☞ **Location:** *Hood River, OR*

This park under construction at the time of printing is testament that if you really want something and work super hard, you just may get it. Known as Lot 6, the Hood River Waterfront Park will be a great place to play. A small group of determined people fought for more than 10 years to construct a park down at the waterfront. They wanted to make sure that the area didn't become home to condominiums, office buildings, hotels and stores. Perhaps by the time you have this book in hand, there'll be a playground, a swimming hole, an amphitheatre and a paved walkway for strolling and biking.

🚶 **Getting There:** From I-84, go North at Exit 63. Turn left when you reach the water and you'll see the park opposite the Hood River Expo building. *www.hoodriverwaterfront.com*

Jackson Park _____4

☞ **Location:** *Hood River, OR*

Located in the center of Hood River, Jackson Park has an outdoor stage, a play structure and a grassy hill for kids to run up and roll down. You'll appreciate the tall shady trees during the hot summer. During the summer, people come to the park for numerous events, including the Fourth of July picnic, evening concerts, movies and other community events. Consider having a picnic here after a swim at the community pool down the street. You can also play baseball at the well-manicured diamond. Public restrooms.

Decked out for the 4th of July

Photo by Jody

🚶 **Getting There:** Go west on Oak St., south on 13th St. and turn right on May St. You'll see the park on the corner of 13th St. and May St. *(541) 386-2383, www.ci.hood-river.or.us*

☺Sorosis Park _____ 5

🐾 *Location:* The Dalles, OR

If you're in The Dalles and your children need a place to run around, try Sorosis Park. The view alone will make it worth your while. Situated on a high bluff overlooking the Columbia River, Sorosis Park includes 15 acres and is perhaps the biggest playground in the Gorge. You'll be pleasantly surprised with the creative castle-like wooden play structures, numerous swings, green grass, trees and picnic tables. You can even walk around the rose garden or try a game of tennis. Public restrooms.

🏃 **Getting There:** From Hood River, drive 20 miles east on I-84 to Exit 83. Turn left onto 6th St. Turn right onto Trevitt St., which becomes W. Scenic Dr. Drive up the curvy road to the park at the top of the bluff. *(541) 295-7527, www.ci.the-dalles.or.us*

Toll Bridge Park _____ 6

🐾 *Location:* Parkdale, OR

Tucked away in Parkdale, this gem of a campground/park has play equipment, picnic tables and even a place to throw rocks into the Hood River. The water, the trees and the higher elevation keep this park cooler than many of the others. The concrete sidewalk surrounding the play equipment is a perfect place for early bike riders to peddle around. Kids can also ride the path over to and around the campground and play by the river.

Jason sliding at Toll Bridge Park

Photo by Jody

🏃 **Getting There:** Take I-84 to Exit 64. Drive south on Hwy. 35 for 17 miles and look for a sign for the park near mile marker 84. Turn right on Toll Bridge Rd. and drive into the park. *(541) 352-5522, www.co.hood-river.or.us*

Wilson Park _____ 7

☞ **Location:** *Hood River, OR*

This small neighborhood park scores high on the scale of places for kids to run around. The play equipment is geared for younger kids who can spend hours on the swings and the slides. The large lawn area is great for a picnic plus there are some trees to seek refuge from the hot sun. No public restrooms.

🏃 **Getting There:** Head west on Oak St., turn left onto 13th St. Drive up the hill and turn left onto May St. You'll see the park on the right at the corner of 2nd St. and May St. *City of Hood River, (541) 386-2383, www.ci.hood-river.or.us*

Other Playgrounds

There are a number of other playgrounds, like **Oak Grove Park** (Portland Dr. and Country Club Rd.), and **Culbertson Park** in the Hood River Heights that we chose not to list, but that doesn't mean that your kids won't like them. In White Salmon, try **Rhinegarten Park** located at Lincoln and Main Streets. In Stevenson, **Rock Creek Park** (at the Skamania Fairgrounds) is fabulous. When school is not in session, many of the playgrounds at the local schools are open to the public. Try **Westside Elementary School** (3685 Belmont Dr.), **May St. Elementary School** (10th and May Sts.) and **Pine Grove School** (2405 Eastside Rd.) in Hood River.

Photo by Robin Dickinson

Chapter 2

Hikes with Tikes

The Gorge is .... gorgeous! It's decorated with mountains, rivers, lakes and waterfalls all waiting for you to explore. When the wildflowers start popping out, take off your rain boots and lace up your hiking shoes. Some hikes are more challenging than others; some lead to waterfalls; some have views; some are more protected from our strong winds, and others are paved and good for strollers. We've divided the Chapter into: Paved/Dirt Trails and Waterfall Hikes. Enjoy!

Oskar and Erika
ready to forge ahead

Photo by Monique Pelletier-Anderson

Catherine Creek * HCRH (Hood River, Mosier, Eagle Creek, Cascade Locks, Starvation Creek, Viento) * Indian Creek * Sams-Walker * Skamania Lodge * Tom McCall Nature Preserve * Upper Whoopdie Trail * Beacon Rock / Pool of Winds * Falls Creek * HorseTail Falls * Oneonta Gorge * Tamanawas Falls * Wahclella Falls * Wahkeena to Multnomah Falls

Paved/Dirt Trails: Perfect for Strollers

Many of the paved trails listed below are sections of the Old Columbia River Highway, also known as Highway 30. Built between 1913 and 1922 when automobiles were smaller and a luxury, the Old Highway winds its way through the most scenic areas in the Gorge and in the world. Sam Hill, who along with engineer Sam Lancaster created the Old Highway, stated, "Good roads are more than my hobby, they are my passion." Some

Photo by Ruth

may ask "How in Sam Hill did they build this road?" We always wonder that when we make our way through the tunnel connecting Hood River to Mosier. It was an amazing feat to blast through the rock.

Photo by Nicholas Bieleiier

In the 1950s, the wide Interstate-84 replaced the Old Highway. Today sections of the Old Highway have been re-paved and some parts are closed to vehicles, like the road from Hood River to Mosier and from Eagle Creek to Cascade Locks. These are ideal roads to hike, stroll and bike. On special days, the old cars come out and enjoy the scenery, just like Sam Hill.

Catherine Creek _____ 8

- 🐾 **Location:** Bingen, WA
- ▌ **Difficulty:** Easy to Challenging depending on route
- ▌ **Distance:** Paved trail -1¼ mile; dirt trail is 2 miles
- ▌ **Season:** Spring for wildflowers. Exposed to wind

Will - lovin' the-
Muddy Water

Photo by Patty Gallagher

Come during the springtime and you'll be rewarded with an array of wildflowers and sensational views of the Columbia River and Mt. Hood. The paved trail with interpretive signs starts with a gentle downhill walk through open grassy areas and ponds. You'll also get a bird's eye view of the Catherine Creek waterfall, or you can carefully maneuver your way down the steep hill to get closer to the waterfall. Another option is to hike the dirt road to the arches which you'll access on the North side of the road. Enter the gate and take the first path on the right. This trail follows the creek and depending on the water level, traversing may be tricky. When you cross the river, you'll pass an old abandoned homestead. You can hike up to the top of the rock arch. Beware of poison oak and ticks. During the springtime, we like to look for tadpoles at the pond/water hole located at the top of the hill straight up from the parking lot.

🥾 **Getting There:** Cross the Hood River Bridge and turn right on Hwy. 14 for 6 miles. Make a left onto Old Hwy. No. 8 (between mile markers 70 and 71). Pass Rowland Lake and follow the road 1½ miles to the Catherine Creek parking lot on the north side of the road. *(360) 891-5000, www.fs.fed.us*

> *Please note: Many of the hiking trails listed may traverse areas with rough terrain. Always hike with caution and keep an eagle eye out for little ones, especially in cliff and waterfall areas.*

HCRH - Eagle Creek to Cascade Locks __9

- **Location:** Cascade Locks, OR
- **Difficulty:** Easy
- **Distance:** 2.4 miles from Eagle Creek to Cascade Locks
- **Season:** Year round. Mostly protected from the wind.

This 2.4 mile paved section of the Historic Columbia River Highway (HCRH) parallels I-84 from Eagle Creek to Cascade Locks and is a good hike with a stroller. You can start at either end of the trail. We prefer beginning at the Eagle Creek Fish Hatchery and walking east to Cascade Locks. That way you can look at the fish before you stroll and eat ice cream at the end. The elevation gain is 65 feet and the road is fairly shady and lush. You pass Ruckels Creek and go through a tunnel that ends up on the north side of I-84. Here, you can play with your echo. Most of the trail avoids the busy freeway. Return on the same road or have a friend pick you up in Cascade Locks.

Getting There: Take I-84 west to Bonneville Dam Exit 40 and then double back east on the freeway one mile to the Eagle Creek exit. The Old Highway trail starts to the right of the freeway. *(541) 296-2215, www.oregon.gov/ODOT/HWY/HCRH*

HCRH - Hood River to Mosier____10

- **Location:** Hood River and Mosier
- **Difficulty:** Easy
- **Distance:** 4.5 miles from Hood River to Mosier
- **Season:** Year round. Mostly protected from the wind.

Clark sees a pirate ship out there

Photo by Karen Bullard

Hood River to Mosier is the most popular section of the Historic Columbia River Highway (HCRH) and you'll find bikers, strollers, rollerbladers, bird watchers and lots of families enjoying the paved road. It's a perfect place for parents to get some exercise while their kids nap in the stroller. During the weekend, be careful of the bikers whizzing down the hill. On the rare occasions when we have snow down low, it's really exciting to ski on the trail and see the ice formations in the tunnels. When you're in the tunnels, look for the etching on the wall by people stranded for 12 days in a snow storm in November 1921. What would you do if you were stranded without a cellphone?

Getting There: Take exit 64. Go south on Hwy. 35. Left at the 4-way stop. Follow Old Columbia Hwy. to the parking lot at the end. *(541) 296-2215 www.oregon.gov/ODOT/HWY/HCRH*

HCRH -Starvation Creek to Viento _____ 11

- **Location:** *Just west of Hood River, OR*
- **Difficulty:** *Easy*
- **Distance:** *2 miles round trip*
- **Season:** *Year round. Fairly protected from the wind.*

This resurrected section of the Historic Columbia River Highway (HCRH) is short, mostly shady and closed to automobiles, though the first part

Photo by Michelle Dearing

Vivian exploring her roots

parallels the busy Interstate. Kids can safely meander the one-mile stretch. You can park at either Starvation Creek or Viento. Logistically, if you're coming from Hood River, you might want to park at Viento because it's a few miles closer than driving to the Starvation Creek Exit. This way you can have a picnic when you reach Starvation Creek Falls.

Getting There: Take I-84 west from Hood River to Exit 56 and head left under the freeway to Viento State Park. *(541) 296-2215, www.oregon.gov/ODOT/HWY/HCRH*

Indian Creek Trail_____12

- 🐾 **Location:** *Hood River, OR*
- ▌ **Difficulty:** *Easy*
- ▌ **Distance:** *1 to 4 miles*
- ▌ **Season:** *Year round*

If you're in town and looking for a quick way to commune with nature, hop on the Indian Creek Trail. It's a trail in the making, with most sections completed. The trail from the High School to Arrowhead is our favorite. You'll cross bridges, throw sticks in the creek and if you time it right, pick blackberries. Some kids like to bike this trail, but it's pretty short. Note that you're not allowed to bike on the golf course pathway.

Charging down the unpaved portion of Indian Creek

Photo by Robin Dickinson

🥾 ***Getting There:*** From the center of Hood River, drive south on 13th St. After 1.1. miles, turn right at the light on Brookside Dr. and go 1 mile to the end. Turn right on Indian Creek Rd, then a first quick left on Arrowhead. *(541) 386-5720, www.hoodriverpark sandrec.org*

Mosier Waterfront_____13

- 🐾 **Location:** *Mosier, WA*
- ▌ **Difficulty:** *Easy*
- ▌ **Distance:** *1 to 3 miles depending on route*
- ▌ **Season:** *Year round. Not protected from the wind*

This fairly short trail takes you around the Mosier waterfront area. A drawback is that the road parallels the freeway where you can hear the cars and trucks fly by. However, the path along the waterfront is stroller accessible with benches along the way and places to throw rocks. If you want more, you have a few options: hike around the wetland area and loop back to the parking lot or cross the train tracks and head up to the waterfall and cemetery. Look for shimmering salmon and soaring eagles.

🥾 ***Getting There:*** Take I-84 east from Hood River to Mosier Exit 69. Turn right and then take the first left, leading you under the freeway to Rock Creek Rd. Plenty of parking as long as it isn't windy.

Sams-Walker Trails_____ 14

🐾 **Location:** *Stevenson, WA*
▌ **Difficulty:** *Easy*
▌ **Distance:** *2 miles*
▌ **Season:** *Year round can be windy*

If you're looking for a relaxing hike that's baby jogger friendly, and kids can safely run ahead while you chat with your friend, then this trail might be perfect. The two-mile loop starts with an open meadow where both the Sams and Walker families' horses and cows grazed. The two families homesteaded in this area from 1903 to 1969. Your hike takes you towards the river where you'll find lots of blackberry bushes. As you meander west, past the cottonwoods and the tall willows, you enter a secluded trail surrounded by old oak and cedar trees. Beware of the mosquitos. There are a number of interpretive signs along the way. Back at the meadow with its tall grass and wildflowers, you'll find a stellar view of the top of Beacon Rock.

🚶 **Getting There:** Head west on I-84 for 18.6 miles to Exit 44. Cross The Bridge of the Gods and drive 8.9 miles west on Hwy. 14 until the second Skamania Landing Road located at mile 33. The road is a loop and don't take the first one at the east end. Cross the railroad tracks and drive for ¼ mile to the parking lot.

Skamania Lodge Trails_____ 15

🐾 **Location:** *Stevenson, WA*
▌ **Difficulty:** *Easy*
▌ **Distance:** *1 to 1.7 miles depending on which loop you take*
▌ **Season:** *Year round. Fairly protected from the wind.*

The Skamania Lodge has three trails that weave in and around the golf course. All are short and partially paved: the Creek Loop (1.5 miles), the Lake Loop (1.75 miles), and the Gorge Loop (1.0 miles). The Lake Loop takes you to a view of the river where you can look for frogs in the pond. Watch out for golf balls. There's also a longer trail which takes you all the way to town. If you go on Friday, we highly recommend building up a big appetite and staying for the infamous all-you-can-eat seafood buffet. Did anyone say oysters? Skamania Lodge also has a family golf program where kids can learn and of course enjoy zooming around in the golf carts.

🚶 **Getting There:** Take I-84 west from Hood River to Cascade Locks/Bridge of the Gods Exit 44. Cross the Bridge and turn right on Hwy. 14. Just before you reach downtown Stevenson, you'll see signs to the Lodge. *(800) 221-7117, www.skamania.com*

Tom McCall Nature Preserve_____16

- **Location:** *Rowena, OR*
- **Difficulty:** *Easy for the Plateau Trail and moderate for the McCall Point Trail.*
- **Distance:** *Plateau Trail is one mile; McCall Point Trail is 3 miles*
- **Season:** *Spring is best because of wildflowers. Trail is exposed to sun and wind.*

This popular wildflower trail is named after former Governor Thomas Lawson McCall (1967-1975). Committed to preserving the environment, Gov. McCall was famous for urging people to visit Oregon, but not to stay. You can hike two trails: the Plateau Trail or the steeper three mile McCall Point trail that begins at the south side of the turnaround, gains 1,000 feet of elevation, has a few cliffy areas and brings you up to a stellar view of Mt. Hood and Mt. Adams. The easier Plateau Trail begins at the interpretive sign by the parking lot on the west side of the Hwy. This trail parallels the Rowena Dell ravine and leads to a large pond surrounded by oak trees and poison oak. Keep an eagle eye on your children especially near the ravine, which is a sheer cliff. In the spring, look for tadpoles and frogs. The McCall Point Trail is steep and challenging for small legs, but the view at the top and the flowers along the way are well worth the hike. Because the preserve is owned by The Nature Conservancy, camping and picking flowers are prohibited.

Getting There: Drive 5 miles east on I-84 to Mosier Exit 69. Head east 6 miles on Hwy 30. *(503) 230-1221, www.nature.org*

Luke and Jenna pondering the meaning of life

Photo by Kelly Brown

Upper Whoopdie/ Ridge Trail_____17

☛ **Location:** *Hood River, OR*
▮ **Difficulty:** *Moderate*
▮ **Distance:** *About 3 miles, but less if you opt to walk to the ridge and turn back.*
▮ **Season:** *Year round. Mostly protected from wind.*

Thanks to SDS Lumber, this hilly trail is open to the public and provides sensational views of the Hood River Valley and both mountains, Hood and Adams. On a clear day, you can even see Mt. St. Helens in the distance. Depending on the mood of your kids, you can hike up to the ridge and picnic with a view and then head back down the same path. Or at the ridge, turn right on the path and hike the single trail through the woods and down to the main road. You'll have to walk back on the gravel road for one mile. Jogging strollers will have a hard but possible time. Bring a jacket as the ridge is exposed to wind. Watch for the yellow balsamroot wildflowers in the spring -- they're all over and exquisite!

Hiking the ridge trail in full smiles

Photo by Mendy Maccabee

🥾 **Getting There:** From I-84 take Exit 64 and drive south on Hwy. 35. Drive 3 miles to Whiskey Creek Rd. (mile marker 100). Make a left on Eastside Rd. Make an immediate right onto Old Dalles Dr. This road will turn into gravel. Once it does, drive 1.5 more miles until you see the gate on the right side of the road. Park on the left. *(509) 493-2155, www.sdslumber.com*

Waterfall Hikes

Beacon Rock / Pool of Winds ——— 18

☞ **Location:** *N. Bonneville, WA*
▌ **Difficulty:** *Moderate with some handholding spots*
▌ **Distance:** *Beacon Rock is 1.5 miles round-trip and*
Pool of Winds is 2.8 miles round-trip
▌ **Season:** *Year round. Protected from wind.*

This hike on the Washington side of the Gorge takes you literally face-to-face — no face-to-fall — with a waterfall. First you have to hike 1.4 miles gradually uphill (2100 elevation gain) through the lush forest to Rodney Waterfall. The trail is wide and reasonably Baby Jogger friendly. The Pool of Winds is a rock bowl that encloses the top section of the waterfall. There's a fenced off area where you can lean into the bowl of the waterfall and feel the cold mist. The powerful rush of wind in your face is exhilarating. While you're in the area and you have more energy to burn, hike up the 848-foot Beacon Rock, the core of an ancient volcano. It's a steep 3/4 mile switchback up the rock. Famous explorers William Clark and Meriwether Lewis named the rock and even slept near it. At the top, you'll have a stellar view of the Gorge. The hike up is difficult, not to mention scary for a parent watching little ones near the edge.

🦶 Getting There:
From Hood River, drive I-84 west 16 miles to Cascade Locks. Take Exit 44 and cross the Bridge of the Gods. Turn left on Hwy. 14. Drive for about 7 miles until you see Beacon Rock. Follow the signs to the campground, equipped with picnic tables, swings, restrooms and running water. *Beacon Rock State Park, (509) 427-8265, www.parks.wa.gov*

Clark and his Dad feeling the rush at the Pool of Winds

Photo by Karen Bullard

☺ Falls Creek Falls Trail_____19

Location: Carson, WA
Difficulty: Moderate
Distance: 3.4 miles
Season: Spring to Fall

Moms and sons enjoying the falls

This is a fantastic waterfall hike because it feels like trolls and fairies are going to join you in the dense forest of fir and cedar trees. The trail gradually climbs 1.7 miles uphill winding through the ancient trees. You'll find plenty of logs to practice the balance beam and lots of big trees for hide and seek games. A snack overlooking the river will keep you fueled and energized. You'll cross two suspension bridges before reaching the misty base of the three-tiered 250-foot waterfall. Beware this is also a mountain bike trail, though a pretty challenging one for kids.

Getting There: Cross the Hood River Bridge and head west on Hwy. 14 until milepost 15. That's the turnoff for Carson and the Wind River Hwy. No. 30. Turn right onto Forest Road 3062 until you reach Road 57. Continue 1/4 mile to the trailhead.

Poison Oak

"Leaves of three, let it be." Poison Oak grows prolifically in the Gorge and it comes in different forms. The leaves can be green, red or both. They can be shiny or dull. They can be spade shaped or more like an oak leaf. The poison spreads through a resin called Urushiol which gets absorbed in your skin and then surfaces as a red rash. If you get the rash, Margaret from Mother's Marketplace taught us to slice a potato and place the potato on top of the infected area. The potato dries your skin and relieves most of the itching. Other's recommend an oatmeal bath and cool water. Some say Zanfel works. Tecnu or rubbing alchohol helps some, especially if applied shortly after contact. Remember not to scratch -- it gets worse.

Horsetail and Ponytail Falls_____ 20

- ☞ **Location:** *Waterfall Alley, OR*
- ▌ **Difficulty:** *Difficult with some handholding spots*
- ▌ **Distance:** *2.7 mile loop*
- ▌ **Season:** *Year round. Protected from wind.*

Located in the most scenic area of the Old Columbia Highway (which we've named "Waterfall Alley"), the Horsetail Falls hike takes you physically behind Ponytail waterfall. Listening and watching the water stream down like thunder is an awesome experience. The hike starts just to the east of Horsetail Falls. Your first .4 miles is a steep climb. At Ponytail Falls, you can turn around and go back to the car or continue on the lush green trail, making your way to the top of Oneonta Falls. There's a classic footbridge that crosses the river above Oneonta Falls. Continue on down the trail and you'll end up less than half a mile from your car. If your kids are tired, have someone retrieve the car while you throw rocks into the river at the beginning of the Oneonta trail.

Dad, carry me!

Photo by Ruth

⛺ **Getting There:** Drive I-84 to Ainsworth Park Exit 35. From there you will drive east on the Old Hwy. 1.5 miles to the Horsetail Falls parking lot. *(541) 386-2333, www.fs.fed.us*

Oneonta Gorge _____ 21

- ☞ **Location:** *Waterfall Alley, OR*
- ▌ **Difficulty:** *Difficult*
- ▌ **Season:** *Hot days. Ideal in the late summer, when the creek is lower and warmer.*

This crazy put-on-your-old-sneakers-and-get-wet hike is awesome, especially on a hot summer day. The less than one mile trail takes you inside the narrow gorge and to the bottom of a 100-foot waterfall. The adventure starts with crossing a large pile of logs and hiking in water that can be two-to-four feet deep. Hand-holding and toddler-carrying may be involved. The hike is challenging, but possible with kids of all ages. Just don't tell Grandma!

Wading through the Oneonta Gorge.

Photo by Jody

Getting There: Take I-84 from Hood River west 27 miles to Exit 35. Go west on the Old Hwy. for 1.5 miles until you reach the Horsetail Falls trailhead. Drive a little farther to the sign for Oneonta Gorge. Park just past the Gorge on the left side. *(541) 386-2333, www.fs.fed.us*

Tamanawas Falls ————————— 22

- **Location:** *Mt. Hood, OR*
- **Difficulty:** *Moderate to Easy with a little handholding.*
- **Distance:** *3.8 miles round-trip*
- **Season:** *Summer and fall. Protected from wind.*

When it's hot in Hood River, head up Hwy. 35 to Mt. Hood. This mostly shady hike meanders over log bridges, through old growth trees, and along the streaming creek where you expect to end up at grandmother's house. The Native Americans felt this, too, since Tamanawas means a friendly guardian spirit. The beginning of the trail has some steep parts where you won't want to lose sight of your children. Follow the Cold Spring Creek bed and you'll gradually make a 400-foot elevation gain to the waterfall. Another challenging section is the field of boulders above the creek. You're almost there. You can walk close to the 100-foot falls, but beware, it is always wet and slippery near waterfalls.

Getting There: Take I-84 to Exit 64 and drive 30 miles south on Hwy. 35. At milepost 72, drive .2 miles and park at the Sherwood Campground parking lot. The trailhead is on the right, close to the river. *(541) 352-6002, www.fs.fed-.us/r6/mthood*

Tips for Hiking with Kids

1. Use "Kid-speak" when preparing for a hike. Instead, of "let's go hike three miles," try "want to look for tadpoles?" or "ready to go press flowers." or "let's make tree rubbings."
2. Bring special snacks, plenty of water, extra clothes, and sunscreen.
3. Consider having your child bring her own backpack.
4. Try hiking with a GPS and looking for hidden treasures. Take a look at www.geocaching.com or hide your own treasure.
5. Play hide-and-seek along the trail.
6. Remember, its about the journey, not the destination. If you don't reach the waterfall, that's ok. Take time to look at the ferns, the slugs, the wildflowers and whatever else you encounter.
7. Consider having your hiker document her trip with a camera or a notebook like Charles Darwin and Meriwether Lewis.
8. Whistles. Not only are they fun, but they give children louder voices. Take a look at www.whistleawaycrime.org

Wahclella Falls _____ 23

- ☛ **Location:** *Bonneville, OR*
- **Difficulty:** *Easy*
- **Distance:** *2 miles round-trip*
- **Season:** *Year round.*

Maya and Kai with their Aunt Sassy

Photo by Ruth

This two-mile hike is a perfect first waterfall hike as it is short and relatively easy. The trail starts out wide with Tanner Creek on the right. As you walk into the canyon, the path becomes narrower and the maiden hair ferns carpet the floor. You'll pass Munra Falls, a small waterfall on the way and then end up at the more impressive Wahclella Falls. If you look up to the top of Wahclella Falls, you'll see East Fork Falls. During the spring, the wildflowers scatter along the trail. If its warm, you can venture in the creek just downhill from the waterfall. Although its just two miles, it often takes us many hours to complete.

🥾 **Getting There:** Take I-84 to Bonneville Dam Exit 40. Go left away from the dam and cross under the freeway. Follow the sign for Wahclella Falls. *(541) 386-2333, www.fs.fed.us*

☺ Wahkeena to Multnomah Falls __24

- ☛ **Location:** *Waterfall Alley, OR*
- ▌ **Difficulty:** *Difficult*
- ▌ **Distance:** *5-mile loop*
- ▌ **Season:** *Year round*

This is one of our favorite hikes because it takes you to a number of waterfalls. The trail is challenging and a bit long (5 miles), but there's ice cream waiting for you at Multnomah Falls' Lodge. The first two miles are steep switchbacks. Follow Larch Mt. trail signs then turn left at Multnomah Creek. Continue for a little more than half a mile and the trail flattens out. The lush scenery makes you feel like you're at Frodo's home in The Hobbit. You'll pass six waterfalls and end up at the top of the grand Multnomah Falls. That's when the trail can get pretty crowded. It's magnificent to peer down at one of Oregon's largest waterfalls. At the Lodge, we usually have someone walk the half mile back to the Wahkeena Falls parking lot to retrieve the car while we savor the soft serve ice cream and look at exhibits.

🚗 **Getting There:** Take I-84 east 28 miles to Ainsworth Park Exit. 35. Continue west on the Old Hwy. to the Wahkeena Falls Picnic Trail. *(541) 386-2333, www.fs.fed.us*

Parking Permits

Many trails in Oregon and Washington require a parking pass. But you need a PhD to figure out what pass to buy. Here's the scoop: **Northwest Forest Pass** ($5/day; $30/year) Includes in Oregon, Bonneville, Bridge of the Gods, Cloud Cap, Eagle Creek, Wahclella Falls, Wyeth Trailheads and in Washington, Dog Mt., Sams-Walker. U.S. Forest Service, *(800) 270-7504, www.naturenw.org or www.fs.fed.us/r6/feedemo*
Oregon State Parks: ($3/day; $25/year) Includes Ainsworth State Park, Historic Columbia River Highway State Trail, Mayer State Park (Rowena), Memaloose State Park, Viento State Park. *(800) 452-2027, www.oregonstateparks.org*
Washington State Parks: No day use fee for the parks, but a $7/day; $70/year fee for launching watercraft or trailer dumping. *(206) 753-2027, www.parks.wa.gov/parking*
Washington and Oregon Recreation Pass: $100/year; this makes economic sense if you're planning on visiting the federal parks like Crater Lake, Fort Clatsop and Mt. Rainier. Otherwise, if you're staying in the Gorge, the Oregon and Northwest Forest Passes will suffice. *(800) 270-7504; www.naturenw.org*

Chapter 3

Bikin' The Gorge

We have premier biking here in the Gorge with lots of quiet country roads to explore. Pedaling through mud puddles or riding all the way up to the Hood River Twin Tunnels makes a perfect outing. This chapter divides into two: road biking and mountain biking.

Peter testing his new set of training wheels .

Photo by Dave Leder

Bonneville * Old Highway * Klickitat * Maryhill Loop Rd. * The Dalles Riverfront * Kingsley Reservoir * Post Canyon * Ski Bowl

Road Bikin'

Bonneville _____ 25

- **Location:** Between Hood River and Mosier, OR
- **Difficulty:** Moderate
- **Distance:** 4.6 miles one way from Hood River to Mosier
- **Season:** Year round. Not protected from the wind.

North Bonneville has 12 miles of flat paved roads that are perfect for beginning bikers. The bike path weaves around the community, giving it a suburbia-type feel. The roads are separate from cars and provide a perfect first ride for your little one who may be gaining confidence with or without her training wheels. We like starting at the Bonneville Resort where you can have lunch or take in a swim (note: swimming is expensive and not always open to the public.) From the resort pedal towards North Bonneville. The first half mile of the trail is my favorite as it meanders around Kidney Lake before entering North Bonneville, which was built in the late 1970s when the old town of Bonneville was demolished and became the Bonneville powerhouse. The small town is quiet and centers around a golf course. Detour to play Frisbee golf, swing at the playground or munch on berries.

🚴 Getting There:

Take I-84 West to Exit 44. Cross the Columbia River via the Bridge of the Gods ($1 toll). Turn left onto Hwy. 14, drive 3 miles west to Hot Springs Way and turn right. Turn right at the stop sign onto East Cascade Drive and follow this for 1/2 mile to the Resort.

Photo by Ruth

Odometers and Bells

Once you put an odometer on your child's bike, she'll want to bike everywhere and keep track of her miles. Bells also keep biking fun and are required in some cities, like Copenhagen, Denmark.

HCRH - Eagle Creek to Cascade Locks __26

- **Location:** *Cascade Locks, OR*
- **Difficulty:** *Easy*
- **Distance:** *2.4 miles from Eagle Creek to Cascade Locks*
- **Season:** *Year round. Mostly protected from the wind.*

This 2.4 mile paved section of the Historic Columbia River Highway (HCRH) is also separate from cars and for the most part away from the highway noise. The section parallels I-84 from Eagle Creek to Cascade Locks. Although you can start at either end of the trail, I prefer parking at the Eagle Creek Fish Hatchery and biking east to Cascade Locks. Novice bikers enjoy the trail because the elevation gain is only 65 feet. The road passes Ruckels Creek and takes you through a tunnel that ends up on the north side of I-84. When you reach the Bridge of the Gods and Cascade Locks, bike east on Wa-Na-Pa St. less than a half mile to cool off at with your choice of Tillamook ice cream or soft serve. You can return on the same road or have a friend pick you up.

Getting There: Take I-84 west to Bonneville Dam Exit 40 and then double back on the freeway for one mile until you see the Eagle Creek exit. The Old Highway trail starts to the right of the freeway. *(541) 296-2215, www.odot.state.or.us*

In the 1930s, the Model Ts cruised the Old Highway.

Courtesy of History Museum of Hood River County

😊 HCRH - Hood River to Mosier___ 27

- 🐾 **Location:** Between Hood River and Mosier, OR
- ▌ **Difficulty:** Moderate
- ▌ **Distance:** 4.6 miles one way from Hood River to Mosier
- ▌ **Season:** Year round. Not protected from the wind.

This section of the Historic Columbia River Highway (HCRH) is closed to cars and an ideal place to bike with your kids. It's challenging because the beginning is a gradual climb up to the twin tunnels. You'll pass a small trickling waterfall, fields of wildflowers (in the spring) and get great views of the Gorge. The trail can be busy with bikers zipping by. We love

The active Gorge family

riding our bikes all the way to downtown Mosier for brunch at The Good River or an ice cream at the Route 30 Roadside Café. Sometimes one parent will ride home and bring the car, but if your kids have strong legs, you can do the whole trip. The trailhead in Hood River has restrooms and a Visitor's Center.

Photo by Claire Howe

🥾 **Getting There:** Take I-84 to Exit 64. Go south to the four-way stop sign. Turn left on Old Columbia Hwy. Rd. and drive up the curvy road until you reach the Mark O. Hatfield State Park. *(541) 296-2215, www.odot.state.or.us*

I can do it! No training wheels!

Bike Buddy

Ready to shed the training wheels? Try the Bike Buddy harness, where you hold onto the child and not the bike. Local Rebecca Hunter, who owns Bike Buddy with her sister, raves about their product: "After working with my son and the Bike Buddy for about 20 minutes, I went inside...only to look out the window and find him riding on his own." www.bike-buddy.com

Photo by Karen Ostrye

Klickitat_____ 28

- **Location:** Between Hood River and Mosier, OR
- **Difficulty:** Moderate
- **Distance:** 4.6 miles one way from Hood River to Mosier
- **Season:** Year round. Not protected from the wind.

Pack your bikes and head to the town of Klickitat on the Washington side of the Gorge. It's a bit of a drive if you're coming from Hood River, but once you get there, you'll have an adventure. The abandoned two-laned paved road was formerly used to haul timber between Klickitat and Glenwood. You can bike the entire 13 miles with a scramble over rocks at mile 7, but we don't go that far. The road is fairly flat and parallels the Klickitat River where you can stop and play on the beaches, pick blackberries, watch the fishermen catch fish or even take your own pole and catch dinner. You may encounter a few roaming cows on the road -- if you give them space, they probably won't bother you. There isn't much shade, and it could be hot in the summer. You can cool off by dipping your toes in the river. On your way back, detour through the town of Klickitat and take a right on 2nd St. until you reach the river. In the summer, locals challenge each other to jump off the cliff on the other side of the river. Successful cliff divers carve their names on the cliff.

Mooing by the cows.

Photo by Ruth

Getting There: Cross the Hood River Bridge and turn right along Hwy. 14. Drive 10.8 miles to the town of Lyle and then turn left on Hwy. 142 and drive another 16.3 miles to the town of Klickitat. Once you reach the town, drive another 4 miles and turn left at the Bridge. Park at the trailhead just before the gate.

Maryhill Loop Road _____ 29

- ☞ **Location:** *Between Hood River and Mosier, OR*
- ▌ **Difficulty:** *Moderate/Difficult*
- ▌ **Distance:** *4.6 miles one way from Hood River to Mosier*
- ▌ **Season:** *Year round. Not protected from the wind.*

This paved road that is closed to cars is famous worldwide amongst skateboarders, street lugers and bikers for its hairpin corners and clean asphalt. Every summer there's a Speed competition where some competitors top 55 mph. For the young bike rider, you'll face a challenging winding uphill for 2.2 miles on perfect pavement. The remaining half mile has not been repaved since it was built in 1913 by Sam Hill to help transport goods from Goldendale to the Columbia River. It is possible to continue up to Highway 97 and bike all the way to Goldendale, but you probably want to turn around and whiz down the hill. You'll have clear views of all the new wind turbines and your heart will beat fast when you watch your little one fly down the hill. At the entrance, there's lots of tasty blackberry bushes and a creek to splash around. To expand your ride, you can bike the 1.6 miles from the entrance of Maryhill Loop Road to Stonehenge. You will have to ride ¼ mile on Highway 14. From Stonehenge continue down the road about one mile to Maryhill Park.

🚴 **Getting There:** From Hood River, go east on I-84 for 39.8 miles to Exit 104 and head across the bridge towards Yakima. Make a left at US-97 for 2.5 miles. Turn right on Hwy. 14 for 1.4 miles until you reach Maryhill Loop Road. Turn left and drive to the parking lot and gate.

Gwenyth zooming to the finish.

Photo by Ruth

The Dalles Riverfront_____ 30

☞ **Location:** The Dalles, OR
▌ **Difficulty:** Easy
▌ **Distance:** Varies -- 10 miles of trail
▌ **Season:** Year round. Not protected from wind and sun.

The paved Riverfront Trail is wide and flat and great for young bikers. The trail will eventually span 10 miles from the western end of the Discovery Center to the Riverfront Park. Today 8 miles of the road is completed and there are lots of fun distractions along the way. If you start at Pocket Park and head west, you'll pedal past the Google Industrial Buildings and see two wooden fishing platforms anchored along the shore. That's where the Native Americans dip-net for salmon. Around the corner, you can detour into Home at Last's Animal Shelter and play with the homeless dogs. Another stop at Chenowith Creek for fish-viewing and rock throwing. The interpretive signs along the way provide educational distractions. Look up and you may see an osprey sitting on the nest by the telephone pole. Taylor Lake is stocked with rainbow trout. By the time you reach the Discovery Center (which requires an uphill), you won't realize how many miles you have logged.

🚲 **Getting There:** Take I-84 east for 17 miles to Exit 82. Turn left on Chenowith Road and continue on River Road for 1.1. miles. Turn left on Klindt Dr. and in less than .3 miles, you'll see the parking lot. Public bathrooms., *(541) 296-9533, www.nwprd.org*

Bike Events

Mt. Hood Classic: In the end of May, early June, the professional cyclists pedal through our valley in breakneck speed, the local bike shops also host a fun kids bike race. When the race comes to town it feels like the Tour de France. Don't miss the criterium!

Trout Lake Family Ride: In June, the town of Trout Lake hosts a bicycle tour that includes a 11.5 mile family fun ride. www.troutlake.org

Getting ready for the start of the race

Photo by Robin Dickinson

Mountain Bikin'

Kingsley Pipeline Trail _____ 31

☞ **Location:** *Hood River, OR*
❚ **Difficulty:** *Easy*

Photo by Chris VanTilburg

This out-and-back ride is ideal for the beginner mountain bike rider because it is flat and fairly smooth. The only uphill is at the beginning. The dirt trail parallels the irrigation ditch and continues about 8 miles to Punchbowl Falls in Dee. Remember it's about the journey not the destination so if your kids want to stop to cross a log, pick blackberries or look for the occasional fish swimming in the clear water, seize the moment. Some of the ride takes you through wooded shady spots, and other parts pass lots of clear cutting. On the positive side the clear-cutting gives you views of Mt. Hood.

🚶 **Getting There:** Take I-84 to Exit 62. Follow Country Club Rd. until it forks at the end. Veer straight on Binns Hill Rd., then left on Kingsley Rd. Go 2.1 miles and look for unmarked trail on left.

😊 Post Canyon _____ 32

☞ **Location:** *Hood River, OR*
❚ **Difficulty:** *Moderate to Extremely Difficult*

Known for its expert terrain and I-can't-believe-anyone-really-bikes-off-a-40-foot-jump, Post Canyon has trails for all abilities, even beginners. For those of us who are just getting our pedals rolling, the area at the top of the hill called Family Man has tamer teeter totters and ladders. We like to start our adventure at Family Man, play around on the stunts and then bike down the Seven Streams trail to the trailhead at Post Canyon. You'll roll over bridges, experience hairpin turns and zoom down the hill. Make sure your child has a gear bike, otherwise she'll skid away on the downhill. Once you reach the bottom, you can shuttle back up to get the car or if you want to spin your legs more, bike up the hill. Another option is to start at the lower trailhead and play around on the single-track. Our local bike shops have maps of the area and there's one posted at the entrance. The trails are confusing and its very possible to get lost in the woods.

Sawyer doing his tricks at Family Man.

Photo by Clint Bogard

Getting There: To Post Canyon, go south on Country Club Rd. for 1.6 miles, turn right on Post Canyon Rd. and park just after the road turns to gravel. To drive to Family Man, stay on Country Club and turn right on Riordan Hill Road.

Ski Bowl Ski Area _____ 33

- **Location:** *Government Camp, OR*
- **Difficulty:** *Easy to Difficult*

During the summer, Ski Bowl converts their ski area into a premier Mt. Biking resort. You can bring your bike on a ski lift and then enjoy an exhilarating downhill ride. The terrain is full of grasshoppers, single track and stunts. They offer guided rides, lessons, clinics and more. Leave your fear at home and bike with confidence. What Mom in her right mind would say that? If you want to take a break from biking, their summer adventure park is also fun!

Getting There: Take I-84 to Exit 64. Drive 38 miles on Hwy. 35 and take Hwy. 26 toward Portland. Ski Bowl is right in Government Camp. *(503) 272-3206, www.skibowl.com.*

Chapter 4

Rockin' Rock Throwing Locales

How about the splashy idea of throwing and skipping rocks into the water? Or perhaps building towers with rocks. Here are some of our favorite places to throw rocks. You might even get away with reading a book while your children are busy developing their curveball.

Tigger tossing a rock into Laurance Lake

Photo by Clint Bogard

Big Cedars Campground * Hood River Event Site
* Hood River Trestle * Klickitat * Laurance
Lake * Toll Bridge Park

Big Cedars Campground _____ 34

🐾 *Location:* Willard, WA

Another favorite swimming hole, Big Cedars Campground provides endless water and rock throwing opportunities. Our kids love to build river rock dams in the chilly White Salmon River. The rocks are smooth and plentiful. Bring a picnic and a soccer ball as there's a big grassy area. The old growth cedar trees are ideal during a game of hide and seek. Note the area is cooler and shadier, ideal on a hot hot summer day.

What an arm!

Photo by Jody

🛶 **Getting There:** Cross the Hood River Bridge, turn left on Hwy. 14, then right on the Cook-Underwood Road for 8.3 miles. Make a slight right on Willard Rd. Big Cedars is 2 miles past Willard. (509) 427-3980, www.parks.co.skamania.wa.us.

Hood River Event Site _____ 35

🐾 *Location:*   *Hood River, OR*

This very popular windsurfing beach has mostly grass with a narrow pebbly shore. As long as the windsurfers aren't around, this is the perfect rock throwing spot. Rocks are plentiful. It's fun to watch the barges maneuver their way up and down the river. On non-windy days it is usually pretty deserted. When the wind blows, the grassy beach gets covered with windsurf gear and that's when you may need to find another place to throw rocks. Try the beach east of the event site. It's a little more protected. There are public restrooms, very little shade, and a $5 parking fee in the windsurfing months.

🛶 **Getting There:** From I-84 take Exit 63 north. Turn right at the first stop sign. Turn left at the next stop sign. The parking lot is on the right. *(541) 386-1645, www.portofhoodriver.com*

Hood River Trestle ————————— 36

☞ **Location:** *Hood River, OR*

Located on the east side of town, this area is where the Hood River Railroad crosses the Hood River. You can walk out near the trestle and throw rocks or even get your toes wet. There is enough sand for digging and building sand castles. Beware: the river can be swift and it's definitely cold!

Getting There: From I-84 go South at Exit 64 until you reach the 4-way intersection. Drive south on Hwy. 35 for .1 mile. Take the first exit to the right and park near the Pacific Power plant.

Klickitat River ——————————37

☞ **Location:** Lyle, WA and up to the town of Klickitat

The shores of the Klickitat provide plenty of places to practice your skipping. The beach just before the Fisher Hill Bridge is perfect for picnicking, rock throwing and just plain having fun. You can hike here from Lyle thanks to the rails-to-trails project (about two miles). We also like throwing rocks up on the closed highway which is five miles north of the town of Klickitat. The road parallels the river and provides great biking and fishing and rock throwing opportunities.

Kai skipping rocks at Bad Boy Beach!

Photo by Tim

Getting There: Cross the Hood River Bridge and turn right on Hwy. 14 for 10.8 miles to Lyle, the start of the trail. Continue on on Hwy. 142 for 16.3 miles to the town of Klickitat. You can stop and pick up the trail at various points along the way.

Laurance Lake———————————— 38

☞ *Location:* *Parkdale, OR*

If you're here to throw rocks, Tigger might join you! The shoreline at this man-made reservoir varies from sandy to pebbly to rocky. Near the end of the summer, the water levels usually drop creating sandy beach areas that are perfect for rock throwing. Camping is free and fish are abundant. It feels like Mt. Hood is so close that you can leap into the air and reach the peak and then dive into the water for a refreshing swim with the mermaid who frequents this lake.

Getting There: From town, drive south on 13th until it turns into Tucker Rd. Follow that to the Dee Hwy. and all the way to Parkdale. On Baseline, make a right on Clear Creek Road and then drive almost 3 miles. Follow the signs to Laurance Lake. *(541) 352-6002, www.fs.fed.us*

Toll Bridge Park———————————39

☞ *Location:* *Parkdale, OR*

Thanks to the November 2006 floods, Toll Bridge Park has lots more beach along the river where kids can throw rocks into the fast flowing Hood River. They can also climb the logs that have washed up on the shore. When it's time for a change of pace, head to the playground or ride bikes on the flat paved paths.

Getting There: Take I-84 to Exit 64. Drive south on Hwy. 35 for 17 miles and look for a sign for the park around mile marker 84. Turn right on Toll Bridge Rd. and drive into the playground. *(541) 352-5522, www.co.hood-river.or.us*

Trying to hit the log at Toll Bridge Park.

Photo by Ruth

Chapter 5

Swimming Spots for Mermaids and Manatees

If you want to get your toes wet or get wet from head to toe, this section is for you. We have some great places to cool off, whether it's in a swimming pool or a classic swimming hole.

Baby Harper out for a swim

Photo by Tim Ortlieb

Hood River Aquatic Center * Kahneeta High Desert Resort * Ted Walker Memorial Swimming Pool * White Salmon Swimming Pool * Gorton Creek * Hood River Marina * Kingsley Reservoir * Klickitat River * Koberg Beach * Lost Lake * Northwestern Lake Park * Punchbowl Falls in Eagle Creek * The Dalles Riverfront Park * Tucker Park * Wahtum Lake

🙂 Hood River Aquatic Center_____40

🖝 **Location:** *Hood River, OR*

This public swimming pool is one of Hood River's best assets. The center has three pools: a wading pool, a warm therapy pool, and a large lap pool. When the white tent covering the three pools is open during the summer, you can swim with a view of Mt. Adams. Bigger kids can enjoy the rope swing, zipline, slide and a basketball hoop. The wading pool is ideal for the little ones to get wet because it's equipped with toys and is only 1½ feet deep. Best of all is the therapy pool where kids can noodle around in the water for a long time without getting cold, as the pool is usually about 93 degrees. The pool has kickboards, floaties, and more. You can buy swim goggles, swim diapers, but bring your own towels. They also offer swim lessons and kayaking classes. Admission: 0-2 year olds, free; 3-17 and 60 years and up, $2.00; and 18-59 years olds, $3.00.

🚶 **Getting There:** From I-84 take Exit 62 south and east on Cascade Ave. and turn right on 13th St. Drive up the hill and turn right on May St. until you see the big white contraption. *1601 May Street, (541) 386-1303, www.hoodriverparksandrec.org*

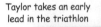

Taylor takes an early lead in the triathlon

Photo by Eric Peterson

Kid's Triathlon

During the summer, the Hood River Valley Parks and Recreation hosts a kids triathalon. It is low-key and a great first triathalon. Participants swim the length of the pool, bike less than one mile and run around the track field.

Kahneeta High Desert Resort_____41

🐟 *Location:* *Warm Springs, OR*

Eighty-five miles south of Hood River in the high desert, Kahneeta Resort is an ideal day-trip or an even better overnight. You can stay at the lodge, campground or in one of their teepees. Owned by the Warm Springs Tribe, the resort has an outdoor double Olympic-size pool filled with natural hot springs mineral water. The pool is gently sloped, making it possible for young kids to stand up in the shallow area. The bigger kids will get their thrill on the 140-foot long water slide. For the adults, enjoy the hot tub and the deluxe European spa and perhaps even make a little money in the casino. Admission: $10.00 for 7 years and older; 3-6 year olds, $5.00; and 2 and under, free.

The big slide! Do you dare?

Photo by Ruth

🏊 **Getting There:** From Hood River, drive south on Hwy. 35 to Hwy. 26. Head east towards Bend/Madras. There's a big sign for Kahneeta, at the Simnasho cut-off. Continue on this road and make a left before the bridge on Hwy. 8. *Warm Springs, (800) 554-4SUN, www.kah-nee-taresort.com*

Ted Walker Memorial Swimming Pool_42

☞ **Location:** *The Dalles, OR*

Open during the summer, this outdoor pool is a great escape from the summer heat. There's a big pool as well as a wading pool that is perfect for little kids to romp around in the water. There's also a playground just outside the pool. Swim lessons offered. Admission: Adults, $3.75; 13-17 year olds, $3.50; and 12 and under, $2.75.

🏊 **Getting There:** From Hood River take I-84 about 20 miles to The Dalles. Get off at the 6th St. Exit 83 and turn right. Turn left on W. 6th St. Turn left on Hostetler St. Turn right on W. 2nd St. *3112 W. 2nd St., The Dalles, (541) 298-2020*

White Salmon Swimming Pool _____43

☞ **Location:** *White Salmon, WA*

When summer comes, try this community outdoor pool for splashy entertainment. Don't forget sunscreen and pool toys! This pool helps you beat the heat and is ideal, especially if you want to swim outside or if you live in Washington and are tired of the trek to Hood River. Swim lessons offered. General admission is $2.25.

🏊 **Getting There:** Cross the Hood River Toll Bridge. Turn left on Hwy. 14. Drive a fraction of a mile and turn right onto Dock Grade Rd. Turn left on Jewett Blvd. and right onto Main St. You'll find the pool right next to Whitson Elementary School. *(509) 493-1419, www.ci.white-salmon.wa.us*

Levi making a splash in the pool

Photo by Terese Roeseler

Swimming Holes

In the summer, there's nothing more refreshing than plunging into one of our natural swimming holes. Here are some of our favorites.

Gorton Creek Falls_____ 44

☞ *Location:* *Wyeth, OR*

Scrambling to the waterfall

This less than one mile scramble through the rocks and water is similar to Oneonta Gorge, only its not as big nor as crowded. It's a great place to go on a hot day to cool off. It's also more challenging and not advised for young children and requires a fair amount of handholding for the nervous mother. The Wyeth area was an early settlement site and was later used as a CCC (Civilian Conservation Corps) camp in the 1930's. The thrilling ¾ mile scamper up to the scenic Gorton Creek Falls is a quick way to get cool on a hot day, not to mention an adventure through the ferns. Go in the late summer when the water isn't as high.

🛶 **Getting There:** Head west on I-84 until you reach Wyeth Exit 51. Go under the freeway, turn right at the Herman Creek Road and follow the signs to the Wyeth Campground. Park at the end.

😎 Hood River Marina _____ 45

☞ *Location:* *Hood River, OR*

This popular ever changing sandy beach on the Columbia River is a favorite place for kids to get their feet wet. You can wade far from the shore as it stays shallow a long way out, especially on the west side. During the summer, when the water is warmer, the beach area is prime real estate for building sandcastles. Shade is tough to find unless you cross the narrow parking area to the lawn with some trees. This beach can be windy, like the rest of the Gorge. Public restrooms are nearby. Warning: Current can be strong and dangerous.

🛶 **Getting There:** From I-84 go north at Exit 64. Make a left at the stop sign and follow the signs to the Marina. Follow the road around past the History Museum of Hood River County, past the large lawn area and park down by the water if possible (free). (541) 386-1645, www.portofhoodriver.com

Kingsley Reservoir_____ 46

📣 **Location:** Hood River, OR

Located nine miles from Hood River, this reservoir attracts swimmers, anglers, dirt bike enthusiasts and campers. Camping is free. You can wade easily since the shoreline is shallow and gradual. Many people fish from the dike just counter clockwise from the wooden pillars. You can also attempt to hike the trail around the lake, but it requires serious bush-whacking to complete the whole loop.

🛶 **Getting There:** In Hood River, drive south on 13th St. which becomes Tucker Rd. Just past mile marker 4, turn right on Portland Dr. Drive two miles and go straight through the 5-way stop sign. Follow the signs to Kingsley Reservoir. (541) 386-3970, www.co.hood-river.or.us

Klickitat River _____ 47

📣 **Location:** Klickitat and Lyle
There are a number of places along the 31-mile Klickitat Trail where you can access the river to cool off. We like the beach, just a few miles up from the turn off at Lyle. The current can be swift, so please take care. Another popular swimming hole is in the town of Klickitat where cliff jumpers dive into the cold water and write their names on the cliff.

🛶 **Getting There:** From I-84, cross the Hood River Bridge, drive east on Hwy. 14 to Lyle and make a left on Hwy. 142. (800) , www.kickitat-trail.org www.oregonstateparks.org

Mother may I try cliiff diving?

Photo by Ruth

Koberg Beach State Recreation Site _48

🐦 *Location:* *Between Hood River and Mosier, OR*

From 1915 to about 1950, Hood Riverites put on their dancing shoes and flocked to Koberg Beach. At that time, this was THE place to be. There was a dance hall often with a live orchestra and other fun festivities. All this changed when the damming of the Columbia River altered the shoreline. The Hood River Historical Museum has great photos documenting the dancing days. Today, the park is a good place to dip your toes and plunge into the river. Park in the parking lot just off the freeway and take the trail to the west side of the big rock. Public restrooms. Parking is free.

Fun and Frolic at Koberg Beach in 1935

Photo courtesy of the History Museum of Hood River County

🚶 **Getting There:** From I-84, drive east to Exit 69 then double back going west and you'll see the signs for Koberg Beach near mile marker 66 (only available westbound). *(800) 551-6949, www.oregonstateparks.org*

🌀 Lost Lake_____49

🐦 *Location:* *Dee, OR*

This picturesque lake about 25 miles from Hood River is an all time favorite. You'll find great swimming and wading spots, a place to rent boats, a general store, lots of salamanders and a memorable view of Mt. Hood. Some of the best swimming holes are located on the trail to the right of the store. These secluded sections make it feel like you have your own private lake. As for the water, it's chilly and crystal clear. Remember to bring bug repellant. $6 entry fee.

A perfect day at Lost Lake

Photo by Sherri Bradfield

🚗 **Getting There:** Take I-84 to Exit 62. Drive south on Cascade Ave. and turn right on 13th St. which becomes Tucker Rd. Just past mile marker 5 make sure to stay right and follow the signs to Dee. Drive 6 miles and turn right toward Dee. Follow the signs another 14 miles to Lost Lake. *(541) 386-6366, www.lostlakeresort.org*

Northwestern Lake Park _____50

🐄 ***Location:*** *White Salmon, WA*

Created by the damming of the White Salmon River, this lake area is a super place to swim, picnic and fish. The lake is also a take out spot for kayakers and river rafters. Kids can wade in the cold and refreshing water. There are plenty of picnic tables, shade, parking and pit toilets. If you are interested in a hike, the Buck Creek Trail System is nearby. To get to Buck Creek, drive past the park. There's a big sign on the road one block up from the park explaining the various trails. If you want to saddle up, try Northwestern Lake Riding Stables located 3 miles up the road.

🚗 **Getting There:** From I-84, take Exit 64 north and cross the Hood River Toll Bridge. Turn left on Hwy. 14 for 1.5 miles. Turn right on Hwy. 141 Alt., go 2 miles until you turn left onto Hwy. 141. Drive 2 miles and look for the sign to Northwestern Lake. Turn left on Northwestern Lake Rd. You'll see the park immediately after crossing the White Salmon River.

Punchbowl Falls in Eagle Creek _____ 51

☞ **Location:** *Bonneville Dam Area, OR*

This swimming hole is awesome not only because of the waterfall itself, but because of the trail leading to the waterfall. You can be certain that once you reach Punchbowl Falls, the water will cool you down! To get to the falls, hike 2 miles gradually uphill on Eagle Creek Trail. Parts of this trail have steep cliffs with cables serving as guard-rails. That's one of the reasons we recommend only taking older kids or kids small enough to be in backpacks. Eagle Creek is one of the most popular hiking trails in the Gorge, so try to go early to get a parking place or go during the week. Every summer, daring kids get hurt jumping off the cliffs, so be extra careful. If your kids love to hike and want more, you can continue past Punchbowl Falls and hike to High Bridge (another 1.2 miles after Punchbowl) and Tunnel Falls (4 miles from Punchbowl). There is another Punchbowl Falls in Dee. It's also a popular swimming hole and challenging to get to. You may find gutsy cliff divers; but many adults, including yours truly, are nervous about swimming there.

🏊 **Getting There:** From I-84 in Hood River, drive west 22 miles to Exit 40. Get back on I-84 going east to Exit 41. Turn right at the "T". Follow the road along the creek to the parking lot at the end of the road. *(541) 386-2333, www.fs.fed.us/r6/columbia/waterfalls.htm*

The Dalles Riverfront Park _____ 52

☞ **Location:** *The Dalles, OR*

When the temperatures rise to over 100 degrees Fahrenheit, many folks living in The Dalles run to the Riverfront Park to swim in the river. The beach is sandy, and the floating dock is a 100 yard swim from shore. Kids can play on the elaborate wooden playground equipment. There's also an outdoor inline hockey rink; and if you want to send a puck flying, pick-up games are easy to be had. If you are up for a hike, there are several trails nearby. Once the Riverfront Trail is completed, you'll be able to walk, run or bike all the way east to the Discovery Center. During the summer, beginning windsurfers get their bodies wet here. You'll find plenty of parking. Public restrooms.

🏊 **Getting There:** From Hood River drive east on I-84 for 23 miles until you reach Exit 85. Go north and follow the signs to the Riverfront Park. *(888) 901-7678, www.portofthedalles.com*

Tucker Park _____ 53

🐾 *Location:* *Hood River, OR*

During the hot summer, head to Tucker Park for a refreshing dip in the cool river. The current can be strong, so beware, especially if you dare to swim across to the other side. It's a fun local spot which feels a bit like the shores in southern Georgia. People gather, drink ice tea and beer and dip their toes in the cold water. Good thing we don't have crocodiles.

Dive in, the waters nice and icy

Photo by Ruth

🚣 **Getting There:** From Oak St., turn south on 13th St. which turns into Tucker Rd. Veer right toward Dee after crossing the Hood River. You'll see the park on the right, *(541) 386-2383, www.ci-hood-river.or.us*

Wahtum Lake _____ 54

🐾 *Location:* *Dee, OR*

Looking for a less developed alternative to Lost Lake, try Wahtum Lake. It's a little more challenging to access as you need to climb more than 250 stairs down to the lake. If you venture there in late August, early September, you'll find lots of thimbleberries and huckleberries and not as many mosquitoes. We found lots of crawdads on the North end of the lake where the logs pile up. Look under the logs and you just might get enough for dinner. The Lake is also stocked with trout. If you're really keen, hike the trail to the summit of Chinidere Mountain. You can also hike 13 miles down to Eagle Creek, but then you have to figure out what to do with your car. Another option is to camp around the lake. It can be chilly as the elevation is 3732 feet.

🚣 **Getting There:** From Hood River, drive south on Tucker Road to the Dee Hwy. At Dee, turn right and cross the river. Follow the signs to Lost Lake. After 4.9 miles, take the Wahtum Lake turn off. Continue on the narrow Forest Road for 4.3 miles until Forest Road 1310. Drive for 6 miles to the trailhead. Park and walk the stairs down to the Lake. Day use fee $5.00, camping $10.00

Chapter 6

Alpacas, Goats & Sturgeon, Oh My!

We have lots of animals living in the Gorge. There are also many farms where you and your children can pet and feed these creatures. On your way,

try playing Animal-I-Spy! You will quickly spy alpacas and sturgeons and maybe even a zebra. Below are some of the places where we love to find animals.

Catching a sturgeon — Who's bigger?

Photo by Peter Marbach

Apple Valley Country Store * Birds * Bonneville Fish Hatchery, Locks and Dam * Cascade Alpacas/Good Fortune Farms * Hood River County Fair * Meadows Mountain View Farms * Schreiner Farm * Spring Creek Fish Hatchery

Apple Valley Country Store _____ 55

☞ **Location:** *Hood River, OR*

We're not sure if this is one of our favorite stops because of the goats or the milkshakes. Some of the goats look so large, that you will be ready to jump the fence and help them deliver. The owners will assure you that they are just big goats that may get bigger after your kids feed them with the goat treats available for purchase. Our kids love

the feel of the "tickle tongues" when the goats feast from their palms. After feeding the goats, you might want to go inside the store and taste all the different jams. And if everyone's been really good, you can savor a huckleberry or marion-berry milkshake. They have shaded picnic tables, and a BBQ in the summer. Did we mention the home-made apple pies?

🚣 Getting There: From Oak St., go south on 13th St. which turns into Tucker Rd. After the 4 mile marker the road goes downhill and crosses the Hood River. The store is on the left. *2363 Tucker Rd., Hood River, (541) 386-1971, www.applevalleystore.com*

Birds, Exotic Birds _____ 56

☞ **Location:** *Hood River, OR*

At James' Organic Blueberry Farm, you can see a Lady Amherst Pheasant with her two foot long tail or examine the Red Golden pheasants who when full grown look like someone painted them in bright colors. Nature is incredible! The chickens have fanciful roosting homes, like a pink church and an old fashioned country store. Artist and owner Ted James loves birds, and plans to have about 400 of them! Open all summer (closed Monday/Tuesday).

🚣 Getting There: From Oak St. in downtown Hood River, turn south on 13th St. Turn right on Belmont. Make a left on Methodist. *1190 Methodist Rd., (541) 386-5806*

Bonneville Fish Hatchery and Bonneville Lock and Dam_____57

Location: Bonneville, OR

At this Fish Hatchery, you can look the old sturgeon in the eye. Sturgeon are the oldest and largest living creatures in the Columbia River. They came into this world before the dinosaurs. Make sure to find 60-plus year old Herman, the famous sturgeon that weighs about 400 pounds -- fortunately, he wasn't stolen in 2007, when someone

The prehistoric sturgeon

Photo by Jody

(probably a number of people) managed to sneak into the Hatchery and take six big sturgeon in the middle of the night. The case was never solved. You can also see and feed the farmed trout and salmon. Walk down the stairs to the right of the spawning room between August and November, and you can watch the shimmering salmon jump out of the water in an attempt to catapult themselves over the 5-foot wall. It's also worth your while to see the Dam Visitor Center and view fish swimming up the ladders. If you want more fish fun, take a drive across the Bridge of the Gods to Washington where you can see the inner workings of the dam. Look for the sea lions feasting on salmon, but that's been a big problem as well.

Getting There: From I-84 in Hood River drive west 22 miles to Exit 40. Turn right. Follow the signs to the fish hatchery. *Bonneville Fish Hatchery, (541) 374-8820, www.nwp.usace.army.mil*

Cascade Alpacas/Good Fortune Farms _ 58

☞ **Location:** *Hood River and Dee, OR*

Cousins of the llama, alpacas first came to the United States in 1984 from South America. Today, they are no longer allowed to be imported and as a result, breeding alpacas has become a lucrative business. The Cascade Alpaca Farm has some beautiful alpacas which you can feed. Listen to the babies hum to their mothers and each other. Each one has a unique hum. Alpacas have a gentle personality, as soft as their fur. In their yarn store, you can see a real spinning wheel and see how the farmers spin the soft wool into yarn. There are two different types of alpacas: the Huacaya with fluffy and fine fur and the rarer Suri with silky pencil looking locks. Good Fortune Farm in Dee also has alpacas and a store selling alpaca products, including teddy bears and exquisite coats for mom -- isn't Mother's Day everyday?

Alpaca mommy sweetly humming with baby.

Photo by Rena Russell

🚗 **Getting There:** To **Cascade Alpacas** wind up Hwy. 35. Turn right on Central Vale Rd. Make another right at Wy'East Rd., then a quick left on Sylvester Dr. *4207 Sylvester Dr., Hood River (541) 354-3542, www.cascadealpacas.com.* To **Good Fortune Farms** take 13th St. which turns to Tucker. Stay right at Dee Hwy. until you see the farm on the left side of the road. *6385 Dee, Parkdale, www.goodfortunefarms.com.*

Hood River County Fair_____59

🔫 **Location:** *Odell, OR*
🔥 **Season:** *Late July*

Ride'em Cowgirl

Photo by Ruth

Thanks to the 4H kids, this is the ultimate animal adventure. You'll see horses, pigs, alpacas, chickens, bulls, guinea pigs, sheep, rabbits, geese, mice, turkey and more. The competitors tend to their animals and are usually happy to let you play with them. Many families even camp out at the fair all weekend. It is also interesting to watch the 4-H competitions. You will be surprised how tame the chickens and goats can be. Go early in the day to hang with the animals. Then return in the afternoon for an amusement ride, a performance and yummy fair food, like the super sweet elephant ears.

🚣 **Getting There:**
From Oak St., turn left on 13th to Tucker Rd.. Make a left at Odell Hwy. and right on Wy'east Rd. *3020 Wy'east Rd., (541) 354-2865*

Some Terrific,
Humble Pig...

Photo by Susan Lucas

Other County Fairs
If your kids love fairs, Skamania County hosts a small town fair in Stevenson in mid-August, www.skamaniacountyfair.com. And if they're real keen, venture to the Oregon State Fair in Salem. It's held in the end of August, *www.oregonstatefair.org.*

Meadow's Mountain View Farms ___60

Location: White Salmon, WA
Season: Weekends July - October

On weekends in the fall, the farmers take you on a hayride where you can pick out the perfect pumpkin and explore the farm. They have donkeys, pigs,goats, exquisite flowers and tasty peaches.

Getting There: Cross the Hood River Toll Bridge. Turn left on Hwy. 14. Turn right on Hwy. 141 Alt. for two miles until Arnett Rd. Follow the signs to the farm at the end of this road. *#8 The Knoll, White Salmon, (509) 493-2358*

Schreiner Farms_____61

Location: Dallesport, WA
Season: Year round

Not too many people know about this private farm, and we only recommend it if you find yourself on the Washington side of the Gorge and need a little excursion. It feels like you're on an African Safari. From your car, you can see elk, camels, giraffes, yaks, wallaroos and zebras. Yes, that's right -- zebras in the Gorge! If you are lucky, some of the animals may be hanging out near the gate. The road is less than a mile. You might want to double this outing with a hike at Horsethief Lake State Park or an adventure to Maryhill's Stonehenge, a full size replica of the real Stonehenge.

Getting There: Take I-84 to Exit 64. Cross the Hood River Toll Bridge and turn right onto Hwy. 14 and drive east about 18 miles. Schreiner Rd. is on the left, just past the fire station. *50 Schreiner Farms Rd, (509) 767-1501, www.schreinerfarms.com*

Spring Creek Fish Hatchery _____ 62

🐟 **Location:** *White Salmon, WA*

We have a number of fish hatcheries up and down the Gorge, and they're especially interesting to visit when the salmon are running. The Chinook Salmon spawn in the Fall. They are the largest of the Pacific Salmon and can weigh up to 40 pounds -- that's more than a young child. At the Spring Creek Hatchery, you can watch the fish jump a few feet into the air as they make their way up the fish ladders. Magically, salmon know where home is after they've been out in the ocean for a few years.

🛶 **Getting There:** Cross the Hood River Bridge, turn left on Hwy. 14 for 4 miles. Follow the signs to the Hatchery on the left. *www.fws.gov/gorgefish/springcreek*

Chapter 7

Hanging Out in the Orchards

Grab your bucket and start picking. Summer and Fall in the Gorge means fresh fruits and vegetables. There's nothing tastier than picking and eating food straight from the source. Here in the Gorge, our farms grow some of the best tasting fruit in the world. My mouth is watering just thinking about it!

Clark showing off his bucket full-o-berries.

Photo by Karen Bullard

Apples * Blackberries * Blueberries * Cherries * Huckleberries * Lavender * Pears * Pumpkins * Raspberries

Apples _____ 63

🐾 **Harvest time:** *August - October*

Apples have been growing in the Hood River Valley since the 1850s when Nathaniel and Mary Coe planted the first trees. Along with pears, apples are the most popular fruit. Some orchards, like Alice's Orchards and Kiyokawa Family Orchards, grow their apples on low trees

Photo by Delphine Trahand

that look like bushes and make it easy for kids to pick their own apples. When you pick, hold on to the apple and twist gently. If the apple is ripe, the fruit falls off easily. Many of the orchards allow you to buy from them all year long. Try these U-pick farms:

- **Alice's Orchards:** tractor ride and lots of wild blackberries. *1623 Orchard Rd., Hood River, (541) 386-5478*

Photo by Peter Marbach

- **Draper's Farm:** They grow more than 50 different types of apples plus sell tasty apple cider. Kids can also play with their farm animals. Always open! *6200 Hwy. 35, Mt. Hood, (541) 352- 6625*
- **Kiyokawa Family Orchards:** One of our favorites because they have the largest u-pick area with more than 60 varieties of apples. They also host a Fiesta Day with tractor rides, piñatas and music. *8129 Clear Creek Rd., Parkdale (541) 352-7115, www.mthoodfruit.com*
- **Mt. View Orchards:** hosts special events, including hay rides and apple cider every Saturday in October. 6670 Trout Creek Ridge Road. *Parkdale, OR (800) 529-6554, www. mtvieworchards.com*

Blackberries _____ 64

☞ **Harvest time:** *July - August*

Many scorn blackberries and think of them as nasty weeds. You might also and laugh that they're even listed in our book. It's true -- blackberries are everywhere and can take over your yard. Moreover, picking blackberries is painful because of the prickly thorns. Nevertheless, we still love eating them, especially with ice cream. If you don't have them growing in your yard, here are a few of our favorite spots. The tastiest berries grow near a water source.

- **Bingen Marina:** Follow the signs to the Marina and you'll find lots of berries near the water.
- **Many of the roads near water:** Just walk or bike near an organic orchard or the river and you'll find some plump berries.

Blueberries _____ 65

☞ **Harvest time:** *July and August*

You pick em" and I'll eat em'

Photo by Aaron Baumhackl

Blueberries might be the best fruit to pick with young children because there are no seeds, and most of the bushes are low enough for kids to fill their own bucket. The good news is that blueberries are one of the most nutritious fruits. High in antioxidants, blueberries help ward off cancer, aging and heart disease. Blueberries grow in clusters and do not ripen at the same time. Pick the blue ones and leave the red and green ones for your next visit. One of our favorite farms, James' Organic Blueberries, has pheasants, cranes and chickens. Let your imagination roam, just like their chickens.

- **Browning Blueberries:** *5164 Imai Rd., Hood River* (541) 354-3760
- **James' Organic Blueberries:** (certified organic) *1190 Methodist Road, Hood River* (541) 386-5806
- **Knoll Farm:** 1170 Methodist Road, *Hood River* (541) 386-6576
- **Nelson's Blueberry Farm:** *5175 Woodworth Dr., Parkdale* (541) 352-7141
- **Two Peaks Blue:** *5000 O'Leary Rd. Odell* (541) 354-1706
- **Wilinda's Blueberries:** *730 Frankton, Hood River* (801) 354-3760

Cherries _____ 66

☞ **Harvest time:** *Late June - early August*

The beautiful cherry blossoms alone are reasons to eat cherries. However, picking cherries is a little more challenging than some of the other fruits around, especially if your kids don't know how to spit out the cherry pits. Some orchards forbid children from climbing the ladders that make it easier to reach the cherries. When you pick, look for ones that are plump and ripe. Cherries don't ripen off the tree. There are many varieties -- from Bings to Vans to the most delicious Queen Anne cherries. If you become a cherry enthusiast, it may be prudent to buy a cherry pitter. Try freezing your cherries, pit and all. We also love drying cherries and then dipping them in chocolate - yum! The Hood River Valley hosts a cherry festival during peak season where you'll find more ideas, especially lots of jams.

- **Alice's Orchards** includes a "gator" ride around the orchard.
  1623 Orchard Rd., Hood River, (541) 386-5478
- **Evans Brothers Cherry Farm** lets you visit their farm animals.
  701 State St., Mosier, OR, (541) 478-2743
- **Kiss Orchards:** *2791 Glass Dr., Hood River, (541) 386-3360*
- **Schmerber Farm:** *79 Snowden Rd., White Salmon, WA,* 509-493-4034

Jason preparing to tend the fields

Photo by Jody

Tips for Picking.

1. Pack a hat and sunscreen
2. Call the farm to find out if the fruit is ripe and ready to pick.
3. Avoid washing picked fruit until you are ready to eat it. Washing fruit prematurely makes it more apt to spoil quicker.
4. Some fruit, like cherries and blueberries, are best picked in the morning.
5. Leave your pets at home.
6. After harvesting, keep your fruit in a cool place.
7. Buy a vacuum sealer or dehydrator to preserve the bounty for the winter.

Huckleberries _____ 67

☞ **Harvest time:** *August - September*

Grizzly bears love them; Huck Finn may have been named after them; and farmers have been unable to grow them. When you search for and find these plump huckleberries, you can imagine the Native Americans doing the same. Similar to blueberries, huckleberries are a deep purple color and a little smaller in size. Most wild huckleberry fields grow in higher elevations. Before you search, you might want to sample a huckleberry shake at the Apple Valley Country Store on Tucker Rd., Mikes' Ice Cream in Hood River, or at the city of Bingen's annual huckleberry festival in September.

- **Elk Cove at Cloud Cap:** This kid-friendly 3.8 mile trail off of Cloud Cap has fields of huckleberries and wildflowers, not to mention a fabulous view of Mount Hood.
- **Gifford Pinchot National Forest Huckleberry Fields** (or Sawtooth Berry Fields): It is worth the bumps over the washboard dirt roads to get to this area. You are allowed to pick on one side of the road as the other side is exclusively for Native Americans. Check with the Ranger Station for status of berry ripeness. *www.fs.fed.us/gpnf*
- **Tea Cup Lake:** This popular cross country area is home to wild huckleberry fields. You'll find bushes bordering the trail.
- **Wahtum Lake:** Not only is this a fun place to go and cool off, but there are tons of berries to nourish you throughout the day.

Lavender _____ 68

☞ **Harvest time:** *June - October*

From early June until October, head to the lavender fields and bring some sweet smelling flowers or lavender lotion home. Lavender is not only aromatic and therapeutic (it relieves burns, bites, headaches, sore muscles and has other natural healing powers), but it can also be used to flavor your food, both sweet on your ice cream, or savory on your lamb. Here in the Gorge, we have a number of lavender farms which produce their

Lounging in a field of fragrant lavender

Photo by Kai Lai

own lavender products. You may find lots of bees buzzing around the fields, but they're usually so full of nectar that they won't sting you.

- **Hood River Lavender:** Located on a steep hill overlooking both Mt. Hood and Mt. Adams, this farm grows more than 60 varieties of organic lavender. They host a yearly festival where you can make lavender wands -- a perfect present for Grandma. *3801 Straight Hill Rd., Hood River (888) Lav-Farm, www.hoodriverlavender.com*
- **Lavender Valley Farm:** Stunning view of Mt. Hood with the purple fields of lavender in the foreground. Lavender Valley also has lots of exquisite products selling world-wide. *3925 Portland Dr., Hood River (541) 386-9100, www.lavendervalley.com*
- **Hoffman Hills Lavender:** (Saturdays only). They have a guest cottage and farm-made products. *6160 Mill Creek Rd. The Dalles (541) 506-2882, www.hoffmanhillslavender.com*

Pears _____ 69

🐛 *Harvest time:* August - October

There's nothing tastier than a perfectly ripened Comice pear (except maybe ice cream or chocolate). Indeed, pears are flavorful, not to mention healthy. Our area grows more than half of the country's winter pears (Anjou, Bosc and Comice), and we produce 11 percent of all the United States' Bartlett pears. Some pears like Star Krimson do not ripen well on the tree and need to be picked ahead of time. However, the Anjou or Bartlett's can be plucked and eaten right from the tree. To properly pick a pear (can you say that fast?), hold the pear and twist so that the stem separates easily from the branch. If you want your pear to ripen quickly, place it in a brown paper bag with a banana. The banana releases ethylene gas that makes a pear ripen. Besides eating them fresh or in pies, try dipping pears in chocolate or thinly slicing them for salads. Just pearfect!

Contemplating the laws of gravity

- **Alice's Orchards:** *1623 Orchard Rd., Hood River, (541) 386-5478*
- **Draper's Farm:** *6200 Hwy. 35, Mt. Hood, (541) 352-6625*
- **Mt. Hood Organic Farms & Garden Cottages:** You can't pick the pears here, but you can buy fruit from the farm or even stay in their cozy cottages. It's also fun to walk around the orchards and explore. *7130 Smullen Rd., Mt. Hood, www.mthoodorganicfarms.com*

Photo by Robin Dickinson

Pumpkins _____ 70

☞ **Harvest time:** *October*

Choosing your own pumpkin from the patch is an annual event for many families. Our rule is that the kids can only pick out a pumpkin that they can carry your own pumpkin! Many of the pumpkin patches host lots of other Halloween activities:

Photo by Robn Dickinson

- **Rasmussen Farms:** Dolly Rasmussen and her staff have the talent to transform pumpkins into all different animate and inanimate objects, including Peter Rabbit and Marilyn Monroe. The farm goes all out for Halloween, including growing a cornfield maze and creating a haunted house. It's a must see for all the local kids. According to Rassmussen's website, nickjr.com rated the Halloween experience at Rasmussen Farms to be one of the top 11 Halloween places in the nation for kids. *3020 Thomsen Rd, Hood River, (541) 386-4622, www.rasmussenfarms.com*

Picking out the perfect pumpkin.

Photo by Michelle Dearing

- **Meadow's Mountain View Farms:** This farm takes Halloween seriously. They have magnificent pumpkins, a hay ride and farm animals. The farm is open on the weekends in the fall until Halloween. *End of Arnett Rd., White Salmon, (509) 493-2358*

Raspberries _____ 71

☞ **Harvest time:** *Late June and late September*

Raspberries grow on vines similar to blackberries. The good news is that the vines do not have thorns and fresh raspberries melt in your mouth! Look out for the golden raspberries — they're the best.

- **Indian Creek Ranch:** This farm grows an heirloom variety of golden raspberries. Their fruit is certified organic and melts in your mouth. We love eating the berries fresh, but they also taste great on ice cream. You can freeze them. They have two crops: one in late June /early July and another in late September. *4169 Barrett Dr., Hood River, (541) 386-6719 (call first to check on ripeness)*

Other U-pick Opportunities

- **Annie's Apricots:** Tasty apricots color the trees of this small farm located a few miles east of the town of Mosier on Hwy. 30. You'll see the sign on the right. Harvest is mid-July and only lasts for a few weeks. *8264 Hwy. 30, Mosier*
- **Draper's Farm:** In addition to apples and pears, this farm grows peaches, plums, and nectarines. They often have sheep and other animals. *6200 Hwy. 35, Mt. Hood, (541) 352-6625*
- **Rasmussen Farms:** In the fall, Rasmussen grows a forest of sunflowers and other u-pick flowers. They also have a selection of herbs, and strawberries which used to be a main crop in the valley. *3020 Thomsen Rd., Hood River, (541) 386-4622, www.rasmussenfarms.com*

Picking strawberries
at Rasmussens.

Eating Local

Fun Food Activities _____72

We are surrounded by fertile soil and hardworking farmers who grow some of the best food in the world. Eating local especially in the Fall is easily possible. Below are some ways to know your farmer.

- **Fruit Festivals:** The Hood River Valley hosts several fruit festivals, including Blossom Festival (April), Cherry Days (July), Apple Days (August), Pear Celebration (September), Heirloom Apple Days (October) and Harvest Festival (October). www.hoodriver.org.
- **Farmers' Markets:** We have a number of farmers' markets around the Gorge. Hood River's is on Thursday afternoons and Saturday mornings, The Dalles on Friday, Trout Lake, Husum and Goldendale are on Saturday.
- **Community Supported Agriculture (CSA's):** Some farms offer memberships in exchange for regular deliveries of their produce. In a sense you invest in the farm and reap the benefits of the harvest. Here are some favorite CSAs: Dancing Moon Farm, Raisin Hill Farm and Hood River Organic.
- **Hood River Fruit Loop:** For more information about local farms, pick up a Hood River Fruit Loop Map or take a look at their website: www.hoodriverfruitloop.com.
- **Gorge Grown:** You can also learn about local farms by logging on to www.GorgeGrown.com. A collective of local farms, Gorge Grown hosts a local farmers' market on Thursday afternoons in Hood River.
- **Fruit Heritage Museum:** Located in The Fruit Company's packing house, the Fruit Museum details the history of the fruit industry. You can see a 1930s pickers cabin and learn about the struggles and rewards of farming. www.thefruitcompany.com

Maya loves the chicks at Dancing Moon Farm.

Photo by Ruth

Chapter 8

Promising Picnic Places

Fresh air, a place to run around and good food are key ingredients to a successful outing. You can picnic almost anywhere, especially in most of the areas listed in our book. This chapter lists some of our favorite picnic spots. Bring a ball, some bubbles, and maybe a few other toys. Don't forget the peanut butter & jelly sandwiches and other gourmet items!

Cowboy Connor ready to chow down in style

Photo by Maura Muhl

Dog Creek Waterfall * Hood River Marina * Maryhill Winery * Starvation Creek * Stratton Gardens * Tucker Park * Wind River Cellars

Dog Creek Waterfall _____73

☞ **Location:** *Skamania, WA*

We love picnicking here on a hot day. The 30-foot cascading waterfall is only 100 feet from the gravel parking area, so it's quickly satisfying for the little ones who are eager to get wet before or after lunch. The stream provides lots of enjoyment. Look for the tiny fish swimming around. The overly adventurous ones like local author Scott Cook scramble up the rocks to even more waterfalls or maybe some pokin' around -- so stay away from that area.

Getting There: Cross the Hood River Bridge and turn left on Hwy. 14 for 9.2 miles. You'll find the sign for Dog Creek just past milepost 56.

Hood River Marina/Delta _____74

☞ **Location:** *Hood River, OR*

Thanks to the huge flood of 2006, we have lots of new dirt piled up at the Hood River Delta. It's a great place for running with our dog, building sandcastles and picnicking. Stay upwind of the kites, and beware of the strong current. The Hood River Marina, east of the delta, is another fun hang-out. You'll see devoted Dads doing crazy things like teaching their kids how to waterski. No need for a motorboat or a gym!

Who needs a boat?

Getting There: To get to the Delta, cross the 2nd St. bridge and make the first right by the gas station. Then turn left down the gravel spit. (fee in the summer). To the Marina, drive as if you're going to cross the Hood River Bridge, turn left at the stop sign and continue past the History Museum.

Maryhill Winery_____75

☛ *Location: Maryhill, WA*

Located 40 miles from Hood River, the Maryhill winery has panoramic views of Mt. Hood and the Gorge. The winery doesn't serve lunch; instead they encourage guests to picnic at their tables. You can bring your picnic or purchase food at their stocked deli. They have a huge outdoor amphitheater for live concerts, which is also ideal for running around and creating your own spontaneous performance.

Getting There: From Hood River, drive east on I-84 to Exit 104. Cross the Sam Hill Bridge into Washington. Go north on Hwy. 97 until you reach Hwy. 14. Turn left to the winery, after the Maryhill Museum. *(877) 627-9445, www.maryhillwinery.com*

Starvation Creek _____76

☛ *Location: 10 miles west of Hood River, OR*

This rest area offers a super place for a shady picnic by a waterfall that's less than 300 feet from the parking lot. When you picnic here, think about the 140-plus passengers on the trains that were marooned for three weeks in 1884 because of a blizzard. Many people almost starved — hence the name - but they were rescued by a group of skiers who came from Hood River. There are picnic tables near the base of the 180-plus-foot waterfall. You might want to bring the bikes and take a spin on the paved trail from Starvation Creek to Viento State Park. Public restrooms.

Looking for monsters at Starvation Creek Falls

Photo by Terese Roeseler

Getting There: From Hood River drive west on I-84 for 11 miles and take Exit 51 (Wyeth Exit). Double back on I-84 going east until the well-marked Starvation Creek Exit 55. *(800) 551-6949, www.oregonstateparks.org*

Stratton Gardens_____77

☞ **Location:** *Hood River, OR*

This wonderful urban picnic spot has plenty of benches and lots of flowers to smell. The city garden is located on Sherman St. between Horsefeathers Restaurant and the Courthouse. If you find yourself in the middle of town, hike up the stairs next to the fish fountain and enjoy Hood River's garden. You'll find a stellar view of the river and signage for all the plants.

Getting There: Located between 2nd and 3rd Sts. and State and Sherman Sts. in downtown Hood River.

☺Tucker Park _____78

☞ **Location:** *Hood River, OR*

Tucker Park is a popular camping area in the summer. Just before the entrance to the campground, you'll find plenty of picnic tables, a sink and a place to barbeque. You can picnic here or take the trail north of the picnic tables that leads to the south bank of the Hood River. Supplement your picnic with a huckleberry milkshake or decadent pie from the Apple Valley Country Store just across the street. Beware of the swift current.

Getting There: From I-84 go south at Exit 62. Proceed on Cascade Ave. and turn right onto 13th St. which turns into Tucker Rd. Just after mile marker 5, stay right toward Dee. You'll see the sign to Tucker Park on the right. *Hood River County, (541) 386-4477, www.co.hood-river.or.us*

Digging for gold at Tucker Park

Photo by Peter Rysavy

Not PB&J again!

Photo by Jody

Wind River Cellars_____79

☞ *Location: Husum, WA*

There are a number of award winning wineries around the Gorge, and this one encourages families to come and picnic on their deck or down by the grape arbor near their tree house. Wind River Cellars was voted the number one place to kiss, so give your kids a big kiss, then pull out the bologna sandwiches. Vintners Kris and Joel Goodwillie

Harvesting grapes

Photo by Kris Goodwillie

have two boys of their own; if they're home, they may show you some of their hide-outs in their vineyard or depending on the season, have you picking and stomping grapes.

🛶 **Getting There:** Cross the Hood River Toll Bridge. Turn left until Hwy. 141 Alt. Drive 2 miles to the end and turn left onto Hwy. 141. Continue on Hwy. 141 for 4 miles until you pass the town of Husum. Go left on Spring Creek Rd. for two miles up a winding, gravel road. *196 Spring Creek Rd., Husum, (509) 493-2324, www.windrivercellars.com*

Chapter 9

Exciting Expeditions

The Gorge is full of expeditions. The most famous expedition was led by Lewis and Clark who journeyed from Missouri to the Pacific Ocean. The explorers reached the Columbia River on October 16, 1805 and took their canoes on a treacherous journey down river. Maybe you don't want to traverse the entire state, but if you are looking for a longer outing, here are some ideas. What follows are adventures that require a little planning and may take a whole day. Figure out how much time you want to spend (and because kids are involved add another hour or so) and get going!

Gwenyth wondering if this frog will turn into a prince

Photo by Ruth

Go Spelunking inside the Guler Ice Caves * Find the Petroglyphs at Horsethief Lake Park * Board the Sternwheeler * Play along "Waterfall Alley" * Go Geocaching * Look Up at the Stars * Explore Bird Creek Meadows * Ride the Mt. Hood Railroad

Go Spelunking Inside the Ice Caves __80

☛ **Location:** *Guler, WA (West of Trout Lake)*
▌ **Difficulty:** *Difficult inside the ice caves*
▌ **Season:**   *Spring, summer or fall*

Put on your warm clothes, sensible shoes and head lamp and venture under the ground to the Guler Ice Caves. These caves are big lava tubes that stay chilly enough to have ice in them all year round. In fact during the pioneer days when refrigerators didn't exist, the towns of Hood River and The Dalles stocked their homes with ice from the caves. Walking through the caves is challenging because the ground is a pile of rocks and you have to boulder your way through the cave. You can explore the mouth of the cave, or you can make your way inside the caves and down the tubes. If you go into the caves in the spring, you'll find tons of icicles and hear lots of dripping noises. Try turning your flashlights off in the middle of the cave and experience total darkness. The cave right next to the parking area is well marked with wooden steps leading you down under. For more caves, take the narrow path just across the parking lot. You can also walk inside of these caves and see where you'll come out. For more geological wonders head up the road to the Natural Bridges that were formed when the flowing hot lava tubes cooled to form caves, which over the years collapsed. The collapsed areas became trenches and the intact parts became bridges.

Exploring the dark icy caves

🚶 **Getting There:** Cross the Hood River Toll Bridge, turn left on Hwy. 14. Drive 1½ miles and turn right on the Hwy. 141 Alt. until it forks with Hwy. 141. Continue for 19 miles to the town of Trout Lake. Stay to the left at

Photo by Jody

the 'Y' as you enter through town and continue for 6 miles. You can stop at the Ranger Station (.5 miles up) on your left and get a map of the caves. Drive another 5 miles and follow the signs to the Ice Caves. To go to the Natural Bridges, drive less than one mile west on Forest Road 24. *Mt. Adams Ranger Station, Hwy 141, Trout Lake, (509) 395-3400, www.fs.fed.us/gpnf*

Find the Petroglyphs at Columbia Hills State Park _____ 81

🔫 **Location:** *Just east of Dallesport, WA*
▌ **Difficulty:** *Moderate*
▌ **Season:** *April through September*

When the Native Americans lived around what is now known as Horsethief Lake Park, some created pictographs and petroglyphs on the rocks overlooking the river. Pictographs are rock paintings whereas petroglyphs are rock carvings. At that time, the lake didn't exist. That's because The Dalles Dam flooded the village, created the lake, and left many of the rock paintings underwater. Some of the paintings were high enough to escape the flood, and Horsethief Park has one of the most extensive collections of these rock paintings, the most famous named "She Who Watches." Once you stand underneath this painting, you'll feel her power. Both a petroglyph and a pictograph, She Who Watches is the largest and clearest painting in the Gorge. To see the paintings up close, make a reservation with the ranger station. Tours last more than one hour and occur Friday and Saturday mornings at 10:00 am. At the campground, the ranger will give you treasure maps to identify the wooden bears, geese, squirrels and other animals hidden in the trees. We like to fish in the Horsethief

Photo by Clint Bogard

Lake is stocked with hungry fish. For more adventure, head to Horsethief Butte a little more than one mile down the highway from the park. You can walk inside the butte and play around all the rocks. You'll see some serious climbers.

🥾 **Getting There:** From Hood River drive 20 miles east on I-84 until you reach The Dalles. Take Exit 87 north and cross the bridge into Washington. Turn right on Hwy. 14 and proceed for one mile. You'll see signs for the park. Reservation required for the petroglyph tour. *(509) 767-1159, www.parks.wa.gov*

Sofia at the helm of the
Sternwheeler

Photo by Peter Marbach

Board the Sternwheeler_____82

🐾 **Location:** *Cascade Locks, OR*
❚ **Difficulty:** *Easy*
❚ **Season:** *Daily cruises from June to October, with a modified schedule from November to May.*

Drive over to Cascade Locks and take a boat tour on the Sternwheeler, an old-fashioned paddle wheel. This journey up and down the Columbia River is ideal when the grandparents are in town. The two-hour tour is the perfect amount of time before anyone starts jumping overboard. During your cruise, the Captain gives you a history lesson, which includes discussions of the geological formation of the river, the Lewis and Clark expedition and the construction of the Bonneville Dam in 1938. Our kids had fun exploring the boat and were especially fascinated with the paddle wheel as it went round-and-round. You can bring a picnic or dine on board -- the food is good! Bring warm jackets even if you think you don't need them and make sure the Captain doesn't run over any of the windsurfers! Tickets are $26 per adult; $16 for kids; 3 and under are free.

🚣 **Getting There:** From I-84 in Hood River drive west 20 miles to Exit 44. Drive into Cascade Locks and turn right to the Marine Park. *(800) 643-1354, www.sternwheeler.com*

Play along "Waterfall Alley" — on the Scenic Historic Columbia River Hwy.__83

Location: *Waterfall Alley, OR*
Season: *Year round*

We've named this 12-mile gorgeous stretch of the Old Highway from Ainsworth to Crown Point "Waterfall Alley" because it has the highest concentration of waterfalls in the world. Along with the waterfalls, there are tons of hikes, places for picnics and streams for splashing and rock throwing. The trees and water keep the area cool, which is especially desirable on our hot summer days. It's a must see for visitors, and depending on everyone's motivation, you may want to drive the section of the highway up to Crown Point or hike one of the numerous trails. The hike up Horsetail Falls to Ponytail Falls is short and impressive as you can stand behind the waterfall. Another short hike is to walk up the path to the Multnomah Falls' bridge. If it's windy, take your kids to Crown Point where they'll have a spectacular view of the Gorge and feel like the wind may blow them all the way to Kansas. If you want to splash in the water, play in the creek at the base of Oneonta Gorge. Go with the flow — just like the water flowing from the falls — and you'll feel like you've experienced the real beauty of the Gorge.

Getting There: Take I-84 from Hood River west 27 miles to Exit 35. This exit is the beginning of the route along the Old Columbia River Hwy. *(541) 386-2333, www.fs.fed.us*

Go Geocaching _____ 84

Geocaching is an adventure game where you look for hidden treasures with the assistance of a GPS, global positioning system. There are a number of caches (that's a technical term for a container used for provisions) hidden around the Gorge. For an up-to-date list of caches in the Gorge, visit www.geocaching.com. The website provides the coordinates of the hidden cache (not cash!) in Longitude and Latitude. Plug the waypoints into your GPS, and off you go, like pirates looking for treasures. The rules of the game are simple: if you take something from the cache, you must leave something in the cache and write about it in the logbook.

The GPS says we're close, but where's the treasure?

Photo by Ruth

Look up at the Stars _____ 85

☞ **Location:** *Goldendale, WA*

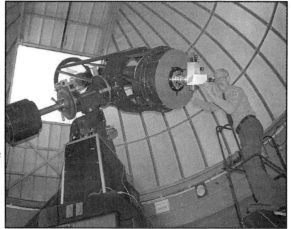

Visit the Goldendale Observatory where you can gaze at the sky through one of the nation's largest public telescopes. With this perspective, it seems like its possible to jump up and land on the moon. If you venture here at night, make sure to have astronomer and host Steve Stout show you

Saturn and its rings. The face on the moon comes in clearly – does it belong to a woman or a man? You and your kids will learn lots about our universe through their educational exhibits and classes. You can also visit during the day and examine our solar system. The whole universe is yours to admire! Plan your visit when the sky is clear, an obvious prerequisite. Hours vary, so call ahead.

Getting There: Take I-84 East for 40.2 miles until exit 104, heading to US-97 towards Yakima. Make a left on I-97/ Hwy. 14 for .4 miles to I-97. Drive for 10.3 miles. Turn left at E. Broadway St./ Highway-142 for 1 mile. Turn right at N. Columbus Ave. and follow the signs to the Observatory. *(509) 773-3141, www.parks.wa.gov and www.perr.com/gosp.html*

Ride the Mt. Hood Railroad _____87

- **Location:** *Hood River, OR*
- **Difficulty:** *Easy*
- **Season:** *Year round*

Got your overalls and railroad hat? Take a train tour from Hood River to Dee and back. The total excursion lasts about three hours if the train turns back in Dee and four hours if it chugs all the way to Parkdale, which will begin again in the Fall of 2008. Seats are assigned, but during the trip you can walk around or get some fresh air in the open-air car and view the beauty of the Gorge. You'll also learn about the history of the Hood River Valley. Mt. Hood Railroad also runs special train rides geared for kids — the most popular being Thomas the Tank Engine. That ride is about 30 minutes. Another kid-friendly ride is the Polar Express.

Thomas pulls into Hood River

Photo by Erik Steighner

Getting There: From I-84 go south at Exit 63. Turn left on Cascade Ave. The station is on your left about one block down. *110 Railroad Ave., Hood River, (800) 872-4661, www.mthoodrr.com*

Explore Bird Creek Meadows_____86

☞ **Location:** *Mt Adams area, WA*
▌ **Difficulty:** *Easy to difficult*
▌ **Season:** *Late August or September to avoid mosquitos*

A Yakama Nation Reservation, Bird Creek Meadows is full of places to hike, camp and swim. We like to van camp at Bird Lake and then hike half a mile up to Bluff Lake where you can circumnavigate the sparkling lake and get a fabulous view of Mt. Adams. Bold ones may jump into the screaming cold but refreshing lake. One of the best kid-friendly hikes is the little more than one mile hike to Bird Creek Meadows and the Hellroaring view-point at the base of Mt. Adams. There's a creek and small waterfall providing lots of enjoyment. In the fall, you can feast on huckleberries and marvel at the fields of wildflowers. Look out for the renegade cows, they're also meandering the area.

Playing at Bird Creek Meadow

Photo by Karen Bullad

🥾 **Getting There:** Cross the Hood River Bridge, go left on Hwy. 14 to Hwy. 141 Alt, then to Trout Lake, go right at the T and follow the long bumpy road to Bird Creek Meadows.

Chapter 10

Extreme Sports for Kids

Here in the Gorge we have more opportunities for outdoor excitment per square foot than any other place in the world. As a result, everyone seems to be involved in some sort of sport or another, whether it's skateboarding, snowboarding, kiteboarding or windsurfing. Extreme? Well, just come try. Remember to pack your helmets, kneepads and sense of adventure!

Becca's smile says it all

Photo by Tony Bolstad

Fishing * Horseback Riding * KiteBoarding *
River Rafting / Kayaking * Sailing * Skateboard
Parks * Windsurfing *

Fishing

Fish on! Be warned -- you just might hook a 10-foot sturgeon or even a 20-pound salmon! The Columbia River has one of the largest runs of salmon and steelhead outside of the great state of Alaska. The Oregon Department of Fish and Wildlife hosts a number of kids fishing days. Make sure to get a license if you are 14 years or older.

Laurance Lake Reservoir_____ 88

☛ *Location:* *Parkdale, OR*

Located about 9 miles from Hood River, this reservoir is stocked with trout and open year round if you can maneuver through the winter snow. Here are the rules: you must tell jokes, eat greasy chips and talk about the big fish that got away!

Lost Lake _____ 89

☛ *Location:* *Dee, OR*

All of the boat rentals include life jackets, whistles, and oars or paddles. Even if you don't catch a fish you can catch some sensational photos of Mt. Hood looming in the background. And if you don't land a fish, look for salamanders.

Deschutes River_____ 90

☛ *Location:* *The Dalles to Warm Springs, OR*

Anglers come from all over the world to fish the Deschutes River which starts in Warm Springs and meanders for more than 100 miles before meeting up with the Columbia River. We have premier fishing in our own backyard!

Reeling in the big one at Lost Lake

Photo by Jody

Horseback Riding

Northwestern Lake Riding Stables __ 91

🐾 **Location:** *White Salmon, WA*

Ride 'em cowboy! This is the only riding stable in the Gorge offering a variety of trail rides. They lead kids 8 years and older on trails through the lush green forest surrounding their land. The one hour Creek trail ride is ideal for kids and exciting, especially in the spring when the water is high and the ferns and wildflowers are out. They have exquisite trails to explore and a summer camp as well.

🏇 **Getting There:** Cross the Hood River Bridge. Turn left on Hwy. 14 to Hwy. 141 Alt, which intersects with Hwy. 141. Veer left for 3 miles to Northwestern Lake Rd. Turn left for .5 miles. Make a left at Lake View Rd. for 2 miles to the stables. *126 Little Buck Creek Rd., (509) 493-4965, www.nwstables.com*

The lush Creek trail

Windwalker Ranch _____ 92

🐾 **Location:** *Husum, WA*

Windwalker Ranch offers various riding lessons during the spring and summer. Owner Kim's horses, some which are miniatures, show their personalities and trust because of the Carolyn Resnick method which she teaches her students. She specializes in therapeutic riding.

🏇 **Getting There:** Cross the Hood River Bridge. Turn left on Hwy. 141 Alt. which merges with Hwy. 141. Drive for 4 miles. Just past Husum, go left on Spring Creek Rd. for .4 miles then left on Lower Spring Creek Rd. *55 Lower Spring Creek Road, (509) 493-2409, www.jcfwindwalker.org*

Kiteboarding

Kids as young as seven years old can learn to kiteboard, but most schools encourage waiting until the teenage years when kids are more apt to make safe decisions while on the water. If your child is keen on kiting, below are some of the places where she can learn to fly through the air and zip through the water:

Erin launching a kite

Photo by New Wind

Big Winds _____ 94

☞ **Location:** *Hood River Marina*

Big Winds teaches kids who are 14 years old and older. They start with the trainer kite on the hard ground before transitioning to the water. The first ride on the river usually starts at Wells Island with a private instructor following you on a jet ski. (541) 386-6086, www.bigwinds.com

The Gorge Kite School _____ 93

☞ **Location:** *Hood River Kite Spit*

This school offers private lessons to anyone who weigh at least 70 pounds. Owner Mark Worth believes that kids with good judgment will recognize that kiteboarding is dangerous, and with proper instruction will learn how to be safe on the water. But he says kids also are some of his best students and learn incredibly fast. *1000 Kite Point, (541) 490-4401, www.gorgekite.com.*

New Wind Kite School _____ 95

☞ *Location:* *Hood River kite Spit*

New Winds has a kids camp for 13 to 16 year olds. They love the fact that kiting teaches so many life skills, including team work, persistance, independence and focus. Instructors follow students with a jet ski. *(541) 387-2440, www.kiteschool.com*

Sandbar: Deltas are caused when a faster moving river flows into a slower moving body of water. In November 2007, we had a huge flood which created 26 acres of land in front of Hood River. The Sandbar is a great place for kiters to launch and it's also one of our favorite places to kid around and play with trainer kites. Remember to stay upwind of the kites.

River Rafting / Kayaking

Want to get wet and raft down one of our raging rivers? If your child can swim, and is ready to hop in a raft, here are a few local outfitters that will guide you down the river.

One down, five to go

Photo by All Adventures

All Adventures in the Gorge_____103

If you're 9 years old or older, this family-owned company will guide you down the wildest or mildest river. Owner Karen Driver guarantees that rafting will build teamwork and an appreciation of the wilderness. *(800) 74-FLOAT (35628), www.alladventures.net*

Columbia Gorge Kayak School_____104

If you are 80 pounds and anxious to take a kayak down one of our rivers, then this school will teach you the necessary skills. You first spend time in the Hood River pool learning how to roll a kayak, and once you've mastered the roll, you can head to the Klickitat River. *(541) 308-0282, www.gorgekayaker.com*

River Rider_____105

A river rider is someone who loves whitewater and wants other people to enjoy it as well. This group takes young kids down Class I and II rivers. *Hwy. 141 near Husum, (800) 448-RAFT (7238), www.riverrider.com*

Wet Planet Rafting_____106

Wet Planet helps 10 year olds and older experience the raging rapids and the calm smooth waters of the White Salmon, Wind River and Klickitat. They also host a summer kayak camp where kids practice rolls in their pool and learn how to read the river. *(800) 306-1673, www.wetplanetwhitewater.com*

Getting ready for the rapids

Photo by Jaco Klinkenberg

Zoller's Outdoor Odysseys, Inc.__ 107

Enthusiastic and competent 6-7 year olds and up are welcome to hold a paddle and float down the White Salmon or Klickitat Rivers. Owner Mark Zoller used to work with UPS, so he knows how to run a tight ship, one that's organized and on time. Their facility has lots of toys, including a lounging BBQ area, volleyball courts, deli and a view. *(800) 366-2004, www.zooraft.com*

Sailing

Columbia Gorge Sailing _____ 96

☛ **Location:** *Hood River and Cascade Locks, OR*

Thanks to Jaime and Andy Mack, young kids can learn to sail on the river, either in Hood River or Cascade Locks. Cascade Locks is known as one of the premier places to race dinghies (small boats). For the beginner, the seven foot long Optimist Sailboat is perfect. Kids learn to sail in circles around buoys or if they prefer forwards and backwards. Watch out for the boom – you know why it earned the name. Classes are held during the summer when the west wind blows and the water is warm. Contact Hood River Community Education at *541-386-2055,www.hrcommunityed.org*

Kira and Sophie cruising along

Photo by Ruth

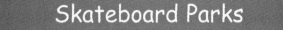

Skateboard Parks

If your kids have graduated from the swings and are now rolling on skateboards, let them loose at one of these skateboarding parks. It's amazing to watch the skaters maneuver the ramps. If it's your child, maybe you better close your eyes!

Hood River Skate Park _____ 97

☞ **Location:** *Hood River, OR*

Constructed underneath the old Cottonwood trees, this impressive and shady skate park has an 11-foot steel half pipe and numerous other obstacles to challenge the wheels. It is also known as one of

the better skateboard parks in Oregon. The park is full of skateboarders of all talents. There are porta potties and picnic tables.

Tae ollying at the Hood River Skate Park

Photo by Clint Bogard

Getting There: From I-84 Exit 62, turn left on Cascade Ave. and then make another left on Wasco St. The skate park is on the right side of the street at 20th St. and Wasco St. *(541) 386-1303, www.community.gorge.net*

Benjamin Rockwell Memorial Skate Park __98

☞ **Location:** *The Dalles, OR*

Named after a local skater who died in a plane accident, this skateboard park in The Dalles is not considered super challenging, but worth a stop. The park has several ramps constructed on an asphalt pad. There are no restrooms, drinking fountains, or picnic tables.

Getting There: From Hood River take I-84 east about 20 miles until you reach the W. 6th St. exit in The Dalles. Turn left onto W. 6th St. and right onto Cherry Heights Rd. Look for the skate park. *(541) 296-9533*

Windsurfing

The smaller and lighter rigs combined with the wide boards have made it much easier for kids to learn to windsurf. Steve Gates, owner of Big Winds and former Mayor of Hood River, says that many parents make the mistake of putting their kids on their own gear which is heavier and harder to maneuver. Another recipe for disaster is to teach kids on the days when experts are sailing on 3.0 sails. It's worth waiting for the right conditions and important to keep the windsurfing experience fun. That mantra helped local rock star Andy Crafts, who learned to windsurf in the mid-90s when he was 5 years old. At that time, Andy and his family spent many days playing at The Hook. "When we sailed, we always had fun. Sometimes, I'd just float on the board." There are a number of sailing schools in town with most lessons being offered at The Hook or the Hood River Marina:

Big Winds Kids Camp_____99

Kids 7 to 13 years old have a blast as they learn how to balance on a board, uphaul, waterstart and hook on with a harness. Big Winds uses the most up-to-date gear which makes learning much easier. Their camp takes place at the Hook, one of the few places in the Gorge protected from the wind. *(888) 509-4210, www.bigwinds.com*

Fun Windsurfing Events

Windfest. The Columbia Gorge Windsurfing Association hosts a weekend in June, where sailors can demo the latest equipment and beginners can take lessons for free. Pray for wind, but not too much! www.cgwa.net

King of the Hook. This crazy event lures contestants of all sorts to the Hook. The search for the king involves creative costumes and bold moves all on a board. Laughter and no shame is necessary.

Andy shreddin'

Photo by Dane Peterson

Hood River Waterplay_____ 100

Hood River Waterplay teaches kids who weigh at least 60 pounds. Students must also be able to swim a minimum of 20 feet before they can start sailing on the water. Lessons take place at Waterplay's private beach near the Marina, just behind the Hood River Inn. *541-386-WIND (9463), www.hoodriverwaterplay.com*

Windsurfing Classes through Community Education_____ 101

The community education department in both Hood River and The Dalles offer windsurfing classes at a very reasonable cost. *Hood River Community Education (541) 386-2055, www.hrcommunityed.org; The Dalles Community College, (541) 296-6182, www.cgcc.cc.or.us*

Windsurfing Lessons through Hood River Valley Parks & Recreation __ 102

These reasonably priced classes are offered for 10 - 18 year olds. Classes take place at "The Hook," just west of the Event Site. *Hood River Parks and Recreation, (541) 386-1303*

Chapter 11

Winter Fun

Winter in the Gorge means skiing, sledding, snowboarding, snowshoeing and even ice skating. Put on your warm mittens and head outside. You'll find that we live in a winter paradise, and playing up at Mt. Hood is the best way to escape the cloudiness that often lingers around town. When its gray in town, you may find blue skies up at the mountain.

A strong snowplow!!

Photo by Tim

Downhill Skiing and Snowboarding * Cross Country Skiing * Ice Skating * Sledding * Tubing

Downhill Skiing and Snowboarding

Outside Magazine ranked Hood River as one of the top ten ski towns. Even though we seldom get snow in town, our mountains do. The skiing is challenging — just ask the National Ski team as they train on Mt. Hood during the summer. We have five downhill ski areas to choose from with Mt. Hood Meadows and Cooper Spur being the closest ones to Hood River. All have rentals and lessons for kids and the price of admission pales to ski resorts in other towns.

Cooper Spur Mountain Resort_____108

📌 **Location:** *Mt. Hood, OR*

This classic family ski area is the closest to Hood River -- about 26 miles away. It is also one of the most affordable ski areas in the state and has one of the best ski teams around. If you've had enough of your skis, try tubing.

🎿 **Getting There:** From I-84 go south at Exit 64. Drive 23 miles south on Hwy. 35 until you reach the second Cooper Spur Rd. Turn right for 2.5 miles to the Cooper Spur Inn and left another 1.5 mile to the ski area. *(541) 352-7803, www.cooperspur.com*

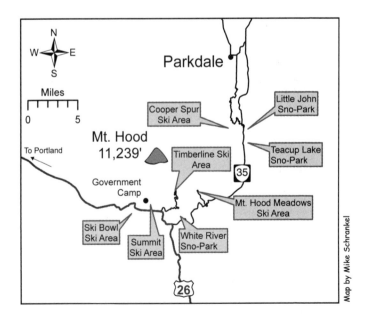

Map by Mike Schrankel

☺ Mt. Hood Meadows Ski Resort_109

🐾 *Location:* Mt. Hood, OR

Meadows' "fun zone" is the perfect place for beginners. Kids ride the magic carpet (like an escalator) up the hill, or hold on to a rope tow to get up the hill. Not too far away, try Buttercup, a gentle beginner lift and in no time your kids will be dragging you into Heather Canyon. When your kids peeter out, take them to the on-site daycare or enroll them in ski school. Snowboard lessons start at 7 years old.

Olympian Monique Pelletier-Anderson teaching her daughter, Erika, to ski

Photo by Mark Anderson

🚵 **Getting There:** From I-84 go south at Exit 64. Drive 36 miles on Hwy. 35 until you see the signs for Mt. Hood Meadows. There are two parking lots. It is better to park in the upper lot farthest from Hood River where the lodge and fun zone are accessible. Many locals park at the lower HRM to avoid the crowds plus its closer to the Hood. *(503) 337-2222, www.skihood.com*

Mt. Hood Ski Bowl Winter Resort & Summer Action Park_____110

🐾 *Location:* Government Camp, OR

Ski Bowl offers the most terrain for night skiing area in America — with 34 lighted runs and a lighted terrain park and halfpipe. In the winter, they have a luge set-up, and in the summer there's an action park with bungee jumps, indy carts and mountain biking. Ski Bowl's longest run is three miles long. Wow!

🚵 **Getting There:** From I-84, go south at Exit 64 and drive 38 miles on Hwy. 35 unti you reach Hwy. 26 toward Portland. Ski Bowl is past Timberline and accessible in the town of Government Camp. *(503) 222-2695, www.skibowl.com*

Summit Ski Area_____ 111

☞ *Location:* *Government Camp, OR*

The oldest ski area in the Northwest, Summit skiers started making turns down the slopes in 1927. It is open on weekends, and has an inner tube hill, a gentle lift and groomed cross-country trails. For the non-skiing parent, the lodge is perfectly situated such that you can read your book and watch your kids master the ski hill.

Getting There: From I-84, go south at Exit 64. Drive 38 miles on Hwy. 35 and take Hwy. 26 toward Portland. Drive 2 ½ miles and turn right into Government Camp. Summit Ski Area is in front of you when you turn off the highway. *(503) 272-0256, www.summitskiarea.com*

Timberline Mountain_____112

☞ *Location:* *Mt. Hood, OR*

Skiing in the summer? That's right! At Timberline you can ski all year round. Timberline is also the only resort on Mt. Hood where you can stay on the mountain, enjoy their outdoor heated pool after skiing and wake up the next morning for some more runs. Built in 1933, the lodge was constructed during the depression as part of the Works Progress Administration. It is now listed on the National Register of Historic Places and you'll see why when you visit. There's a huge fireplace, a number of restaurants and several exhibits about the construction of the lodge. During the summer, you can ski with the national ski team. If you're real serious, they have a number of summer ski camps to keep you in shape and ready for any hill.

Getting There: From I-84, go south at Exit 64. Drive 38 miles on Hwy. 35 and take Hwy. 26 toward Portland. Drive 2 miles until you find turn right on the road to Timberline. Follow the road to the resort. If you get to the town of Government Camp, you've gone too far. *(503) 622-7979, www.timberlinelodge.com*

Ski Area and Sno-Park Parking Permits

Many of the ski and sledding areas are plowed by the Oregon Department of Transportation and thus require a Sno-Park permit. You can buy a permit at the Department of Motor Vehicle offices, Forest Service offices, ski resorts and some sporting goods stores. *www.fs.fed.us* and *www.parks.wa.gov/winter/permits.asp*

Cross Country Skiing

For those who want to avoid the crowds of a downhill ski resort yet desire to get out in the wilderness, cross country skiing may be your answer. We've had some memorable days out in the wild. Below are some of the groomed areas.

Mt. Hood Meadows Ski Resort___ 113

☞ **Location:** *Mt. Hood, OR*

The Nordic Center located at Mt. Hood Meadows' lower lot, has 15 kilometers of groomed trails plus a hut to stow gear, wax skis and warm up with hot chocolate. You can rent skis and take lessons.

Getting There: From I-84, go south at Exit 64. Drive 36 miles on Hwy. 35 until you see the signs for Mt. Hood Meadows. Park in the first lot. *(503) 337-2222, www.skihood.com*

Mt. Adams Recreation Area_____ 114

☞ **Location:** *Trout Lake and Stevenson, WA*

Washington's Gifford Pinchot National Forest divides into five areas, with Mt. Adams and Wind River being the closest. The Forest Service grooms miles of trails north of Trout Lake and in the Wind River area, near the town of Stevenson. Locals love the Old Man Pass Area with 32 miles of trails. The grooming of trails is done rather infrequently. Contact the Forest Service for detailed information. *(360) 891-5001, www.fs.fed.us/gpnf*

Cooper Spur_____ 115

☞ **Location:** *Mt. Hood, OR*

This area has 6.5 kilometers of groomed trails. When the sun is out and the snow just right, you can ski with a beautiful view of the mountain and enjoy lunch and hot chocolate at the Inn. Don't forget your sunscreen. Ski and snowshoe rentals are available at the lodge.

Getting There: From I-84 go south at Exit 64. Drive 23 miles south on Hwy. 35, and right at (the 2nd) Cooper Spur Rd. 2.5 miles. to the Inn. *(541) 352-7803, www.cooperspur.com*

Tea Cup Lake Sno-Park _____ 116

☛ **Location:** *Mt. Hood, OR*

This area has 20 kilometers or 12 miles of groomed trails for both skating and classic skiing. The newly built heated wooden cabin is ideal to warm up, drink some hot chocolate and tell stories.

🎿 **Getting There:** From Hood River, drive 35 miles south on Hwy. 35. The ski area is 1 mile before the Mt. Hood Meadows Resort turn-off. *www.teacupnordic.org*

Trout Lake High School _____ 117

☛ **Location:** *Trout Lake, OR*

2008 was the first year the Trout Lake High School had a groomed track thanks to the generosity of the farm behind the school. The big wide open space and flat terrain sets the scene for an easy and tame family outing.

🎿 **Getting There:** Cross the Hood River Toll Bridge, turn left on Hwy. 14. Drive 1½ miles and turn right on the Hwy. 141 Alt. until it merges with Hwy. 141. Turn left and continue for 19 miles until you reach Trout Lake High School on the right.

Kicking and gliding

Photo by Tim

Trillium Lake Basin _____ 118

☛ **Location:** *Gov't Camp, OR*

Located a few miles from Government Camp, the Trillium Lake area has miles of groomed trails. For a fun family outing, you can rent a cabin, but you have to ski a mile or so to get there.

🎿 **Getting There:** From Hood River, drive south on Hwy. 35. Then east on Hwy. 26. Look for the Sno-park on the left before Government Camp.

Other Cross Country Ski Areas to Explore

The beauty of cross country skiing is that you can ski almost anywhere, escape the crowds and you can usually bring your dog. We like skijoring with our dog, Jedi. A few of our favorite

areas around Mt. Hood are Pocket Creek, Bennett Pass and Laurance Lake. Near Mt. Adams, the trails to Pine Side are sometimes groomed. Check with the Ranger Districts for maps. *(541) 352-6002, www.fs.fed.us/ r6/mthood; Gifford Pinchot National Forest, (360) 891-5000,*

Ice Skating

Perhaps someday we'll have an ice skating rink in the Gorge, but in the meanwhile if its cold and dry enough, there are a few places that ice up. Make sure the ice is safe and thick before exploring. The over-flow mud puddle outside the Hood River Expo Center sometimes freezes and that's a great place to begin. The Bingen Marina has some spots that ice up as well as Balch Lake in Lyle. We've had some magical days up at Laurance Lake in Parkdale where folks play hockey and you can skate around the whole lake.

Erika Skatin' in the Hood.

Photo by Monique

Ice Skating Rinks _____ 119

- **Vancouver: Mt.View Ice Skating Rink**, *14313 SE Mill Plain Blvd., Vancouver, WA, (360) 896-8700, www.mtviewice.com*
- **Lloyd Center Ice Rink** – The rink can be crowded, but you can shop in the mall and do the Hokey Pokey at the same time. *953 Lloyd Center, Portland (503) 288-6073, www.lloydcenterice.com*

Sledding

Sam, the human sled.

Photo by Peter Rysavy

Little John Sno-Park_____ 120

☞ *Location:* *Mt. Hood, OR*

This Sno-Park has four sledding paths and when there's snow, they are full of kids whizzing down the hill. The BIGGEST hill is 600 feet long — that's a long way to climb up and sled down. Steel-runner sleds are prohibited. Little John is well equipped with restrooms and a warming hut with a wood burning stove. If you want to hike or cross country ski, try the trail on the left side of the park. Snow mobiles like the trail as well so it may be a little noisy.

Getting There: From I-84 in Hood River, go south at Exit 64. Drive south on Hwy. 35 about 33 miles. The Sno-park is well marked between mile markers 70 and 71.

White River West Sno-Park _____ 121

☞ *Location:* *Mt. Hood, OR*

This is a popular sledding hill, especially amongst Portlanders. The sledding paths are exhilarating. It's abut a mile walk to the hill, but worth it!

Getting There: From I-84 in Hood River, go south at Exit 64. Drive 34 miles south on Hwy. 35. The sledding hill and parking lot are on the right side of the road. If you get to Hwy. 26 you've gone 4 miles too far.

Tubing

Whooping down the hill on a tube can be an enormous rush. Although our kids could tube forever, we leave when their clothes are soaked or the hill shuts down.

Cooper Spur Mountain Resort_____122

☞ *Location:* *Mt. Hood, OR*

This family resort has two tubing runs; the lower and the extreme! You must be at least 42 inches tall to tube down the mountain.

🛷 **Getting There:** From I-84 go south at Exit 64. Drive 23 miles south on Hwy. 35 until you see the signs for Cooper Spur (passing by the first intersection with Cooper Spur Rd. in the community of Mt. Hood). Take a right on Forest Rd. 3510 and drive 2 ½ miles. *(541) 352-7803, www.cooperspur.com*

Mt. Hood Ski Bowl Winter Resort & Summer Action Park _____123

☞ *Location:* *Government Camp, OR*

Skibowl offers tubing and extreme tubing (yikes!), in the summer and the winter. The easier tubing hill is very wide and not very steep so your kids won't get scared. They also have an indoor super play zone where kids can crawl, bounce, climb and slide.

🛷 **Getting There:** From I-84, go south at Exit 64 and drive 38 miles on Hwy. 35 and take Hwy. 26 toward Portland. Skibowl is past Timberline and is in the town of Government Camp. *(503) 222-2695, www.skibowl.com*

Summit Ski Area _____124

☞ *Location:* *Government Camp, OR*

During the weekend, you can tube down the hills. Summit has two sledding areas: one at the resort and another hill called Snow Bunny that is located 1 ½ miles east of the Timberline Junction on Hwy. 26.

🛷 **Getting There:** From I-84, go south at Exit 64. Drive 38 miles on Hwy. 35 and take Hwy. 26 toward Portland. Drive 2 ½ miles and turn right into Government Camp. Look for the ski area. *(503) 272-0256, www.summitskiarea.com*

Chapter 12

Windsurfing/Kiting Spots For You and Your Tots

Windsurfing can be a great family outing. The key to success is to pick a spot where parents love the sailing and kids enjoy the shore. We've rated the places on a scale from 1 to 5 in terms of wind protection and windsurfing difficulty. We've also added kiting spots, but be sure kids play safely upwind of kite launch areas.

Wind Protection - ability to get out of the wind
(Your living room scores a 5)

Windsurfing Difficulty - considers skill level
(The famous Hatchery scores a 5)

Baby on board at the Event Site.

Photo by Ruth

The Hatchery * Hood River Event Site * Hood River Marina * Home Valley * Maryhill State Park * Roosevelt Park * Rowena * Stevenson

The Hatchery_____ 125

🔖 **Location:** White Salmon, WA
❚ **Wind Protection:** 😊
❚ **Windsurfing Difficulty:** 😊 😊 😊 😊 😊

The Hatchery is The with a capital "T" place for expert windsurfers and kiters to show off their loops and flips. The swell can be gigantic and the wind fierce. It's an exciting place. Kids like to tuck into the woods and play along the shore where there is some wind protection and lots of blackberries. You can also visit the fish hatchery and learn about our salmon. Parking $3/day or $50 summer pass.

🏄 **Getting There:** Cross the Hood River Bridge, make a left on Hwy. 14 and drive 4 miles until you reach the Hatchery.

Hood River Event Site _____ 126

🔖 **Location:** Hood River, OR
❚ **Wind Protection:** 😊
❚ **Windsurfing Difficulty:** 😊 😊

This is one of the closest windsurf beaches (kiters are not allowed, but can access the kite beach across the way) to Hood River and usually has the most kids around as well. You'll be happy with the huge lawn, restrooms, picnic tables, bleacher seats and large parking lot. Your kids will enjoy throwing rocks into the water here or right around the corner on the shore of the Hood River or in the new Waterfront Park just down the beach. Be wary of loads of windsurfing gear and windsurfers maneuvering their equipment. Parking costs $5/day or $50 summer pass.

Photo by Karen Bullard

🏄 **Getting There:** From I-84 go north at Exit 63. Turn right at the stop sign. Turn left at the next stop sign. The parking lot is on the right. *(541) 386-1645, www.portofhoodriver.com*

Hood River Marina _____ 127

- **Location:** *Hood River, OR*
- **Wind Protection:**
- **Windsurfing Difficulty:**

Many beginning and intermediate windsurfers sail at the Marina because the shallow areas make it optimum for mastering water starts. It's also ideal for kids who can happily build sand castles or wade in the shallow water. Beware of the strong current in the middle. You can seek shelter from the wind on the west side of the beach or in the grassy area behind the beach. You'll find an even more protected lawn with trees just across the narrow parking lot. If you want to add a little culture to your outing, walk to the Hood River Museum south of the beach. You can also follow the paved path around the marina and under the bridge. Parking is free.

Getting There: Go north at Exit 64. Make a left at the stop sign just before the Hood River Bridge and follow the signs to the Marina. Follow the road past the museum and the large lawn area. *(541) 386-1645, www.portofhoodirver.com*

Home Valley _____ 128

- **Location:** *6 miles east of Stevenson, WA*
- **Wind Protection:**
- **Windsurfing Difficulty:**

This sailing spot and campground has a protected beach that is shallow and exciting for kids. There's also a baseball diamond and buckets of blackberries in the summer. For the windsurfer and kiter, the grassy area makes rigging easier and you can sail here when the wind is blowing from the east or the west. No parking fee or permit required for day use, but there is a camping fee.

Getting There: From I-84 go north at Exit 64. Cross the bridge and drive 14 miles east on Hwy. 14. You'll see signs for Home Valley. *(509) 427-9478, www.skamaniacounty.org*

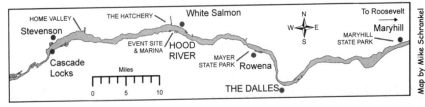

 Maryhill State Park _____ 129

📍 Location: *Goldendale, WA*
❚ Wind Protection: 😊 😊 😊 😊
❚ Windsurfing Difficulty: 😊 😊 😊 😊

This challenging windsurfing spot is ideal for kids. It has a roped off swimming area, a big grassy lawn, biking paths, restrooms, showers and comfortable camping. The beach contains big smooth stones, perfect for skipping rocks. If you want to detour from the beach, you can walk down the road to get peaches or hike up to the Stonehenge replica built by entrepreneur Sam Hill as a memorial to the soldiers from Klickitat County who died in World War I. For the windsurfer, warning: the bridge makes it tough to see barges. The current can be strong. Parking $5/day or buy a Washington State Park pass for $50.

🚣 Getting There: From I-84 drive east to Exit 104, Biggs junction. Cross the bridge and drive one mile north on Hwy. 97. Take the first right and follow the signs to Maryhill. *(360) 902-8844, www.parks.wa.gov*

Want to know where it's windy?
To obtain daily wind conditions and forecasts, take a look at *www.iwindsurf.com and www.nwkite.com* or listen to 104.5 fm.

Roosevelt Park _____130

🐾 **Location:** *Roosevelt, WA*
▌ **Wind Protection:** 😊 😊 😊 😊
▌ **Windsurfing Difficulty:** 😊 😊 😊

Located about one and a half hours east of Hood River, Roosevelt is an ideal place to camp out and sail or kite. Make sure to check the wind report before heading out. There's a big lawn, shady areas, restrooms, camping facilities and even a swing set. On your way, pick up some Maryhill peaches and pack food because there are few amenities nearby. Parking is free, but the lot fills up quickly.

🌲 **Getting There:** From Hood River, take I-84 east 40 miles until Exit 104 and drive across the Sam Hill Bridge into Washington. Drive straight to Hwy. 14. At the top of the hill turn right at the stop sign and drive east for about 33 miles to Roosevelt. Turn right into Roosevelt Park near milepost 133. *(541) 386-9225*

Rowena - Mayer State Park _____131

🐾 **Location:** *Rowena, OR*
▌ **Wind Protection:** 😊 😊 😊
▌ **Windsurfing Difficulty:** 😊 😊 😊

This is another popular spot for families and rightly so because it usually has good wind and lots of places to explore. You'll find restrooms, picnic tables, a large rocky beach and areas that are protected from the wind. Our kids like to hang out around the trees, but it's also fun to play on the volcanic rock away from the windsurfers. Parking is $3 for the day, or $25 for a State Park season pass.

🌲 **Getting There:** From Hood River, drive east on I-84 for 12 miles to Rowena. Take Exit 76, drive under the freeway across the railroad tracks and turn right until you reach the end of the road. *(800) 551-6949, www.oregonstateparks.org*

Other places to windsurf:

To learn more about the places to windsurf in the Gorge, stop into one of our many windsurfing stores, go online to www.windance.com or pick up a copy of the *The Gorge Guide*.

😄 Stevenson _____132

🔫 **Location:** *Stevenson, WA*
▮ **Wind Protection:**   😊 😊 😊 😊
▮ **Windsurfing Difficulty:**   😊 😊

Though the wind might not be as strong as the other areas, the set-ting is family-friendly. This is also the place to sail on East wind days. There's a sloping lawn that is protected from the wind and has trees for shade. Other amenities include a changing room, and clean rest-rooms near-by. You'll find many regulars enjoying this site. From the lawn, you can easily watch the sailors come and go and kids love to throw rocks from the cozy beach. If you are tired of sailing and hang-ing out, stroll along the waterfront or walk into town. Parking is free, but the lot can fill up fast. The kiting launch is a third of a mile east near the boat ramp and beach.

🚤 **Getting There:** Cross the Hood River Bridge turn left on Hwy. 14 for 20 miles until you reach Stevenson. Take a left at any street in the middle of town and cross the railroad tracks. You can also get to Stevenson from the Bridge of the Gods in Cascade Locks, but then you miss watching the windsurfers and kiters along the way. *(509) 427-8265*

Enjoying a great day
at Stevenson

Photo by Ruth

Chapter 13

Indoor Fun Independent Of Sun

Looking for indoor activities where you can stay dry on rainy days and avoid a sunburn on sunny days? How about going to a museum, attending story time at the library, enrolling your kids in classes, painting pots or even bowling? Take a look at the Gorgekids.com website or the Hood River News newspaper.

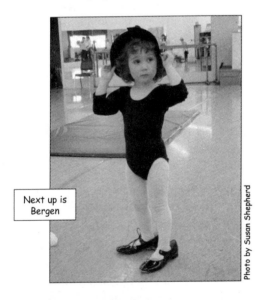

Next up is Bergen

Photo by Susan Shepherd

Libraries * Museums * Playgroups * Kid Classes

Libraries

Hood River Public Library_____133

📣 **Location:** *Hood River, OR*
🚩 **Hours:** *Closed Sundays*

Our library is one of the biggest buildings in town, and it's one of our favorite places to frequent, especially on a rainy day. The new building has a large children's section and a separate room ideal for storytime and other activities. The friendly librarians are always full of ideas and they tell stories on Wednesday and Thursday mornings.

🚶 **Getting There:** From I-84 go south at Exit 63. Turn right on State St. *502 State St., (541) 386-2535, community.gorge.net/libraries/hoodriver*

Stevenson Community Library_____134

📣 **Location:** *Stevenson, WA*
🚩 **Hours:** *Closed Sunday and Monday*

Stevenson Library seems to always have some interesting event for children whether its the annual parade of poetry or story time. Story time is Wedenesday and Thursday mornings at 10:30.

🚶 **Getting There:** Cross the Hood River Bridge and turn left on Hwy. 14. until Columbia Ave. in Stevenson. Turn right and the library is on the corner. 120 NW Vancouver Ave., *(509) 427-5471, www.fvrl.org*

White Salmon Public Library_____135

📣 **Location:** *White Salmon, WA*
🚩 **Hours:** *Closed Sunday and Monday.*

The children's story time at this library is outstanding, and often includes a special art craft. They host a separate story time for kids under three. It's a great place to meet other parents and compare notes about the joys of parenting. Story time is Wednesday mornings

🚶 **Getting There:** Cross the Hood River Bridge and go right on Hwy. 14 into the town of Bingen. Turn left on Hwy. 141/ E. Jewitt Blvd. and drive up the hill. Turn right on Wauna Ave. *#5 Town & Country Square, White Salmon, (509) 493-1132, www.fvrl.org*

Museums

Bonneville Dam/Fish Hatchery___136

☛ Location: *Cascade Locks, OR and North Bonneville, WA*
⌛ Hours: *Open daily 9:00 to 5:00 pm*

The Bonneville Dam Visitor Center in both states has movies and displays about the dam and the various fish, especially the salmon. You can watch the fish swim by the windows looking into the fish ladder; in Washington you can learn about hydo-electric power.

⛴ Getting There: From I-84 in Hood River drive west about 22 miles to Exit 40. Turn right. Follow the signs to the Dam. *(541) 374-8820, www.nwp.usace.army.mil/op/b*

⊙Columbia Gorge Discovery Center_137

☛ Location: *The Dalles, OR*
⌛ Hours: *Open daily, 9:00 to 5:00 pm*

This extraordinary museum focuses on the natural and cultural history of the Gorge. They have a new live raptor exhibit. Another exhibit helps you understand the challenges facing the pioneers on the Oregon Trail -- should they navigate the Columbia River or traverse the Barlow trail? Taking you back to he mid-1800s, you hear about the Columbia River when it was sparkling clear, and full of salmon. Kids love playing on the windsurfer and jumping the waves. It's also fun to try on clothes from the 1800s when Lewis and Clark came through our area. Admission. $8 for adults; $4 for kids 6-16.

Beware Lewis and Clark!

Photo by Discovery Center

🚗 **Getting There:** From Hood River, take I-84 east 20 miles to Exit 82, the first exit in The Dalles. Drive west on West Second St. to Crate's Point access road. Follow the road to the museum parking lot. *5000 Discovery Dr., (541) 296-8600, www.gorgediscovery.org*

Columbia Gorge Interpretive Center_138

📍 ***Location:*** Stevenson, WA
🕐 ***Hours:*** Open daily, 10:00 to 5:00 pm

This museum has life size exhibits that will keep your kids entertained and even educate them about the Gorge. You'll see a 37-foot replica of a fish wheel and get to make your own pictographs. There's an exceptional movie featuring the cataclysmic creation of the Gorge with dramatic pictures. The train outside allows you to explore a real steam engine --- very exciting for the train lover in your family. Admission is $7 for adults; $5 for kids 6-12; free for kids under six.

🚗 **Getting There:** From Hood River, take I-84 west 20 miles to Cascade Locks. Cross the Bridge of the Gods and drive 1.5 miles east on Hwy. 14 to the museum. *990 SW Rock Creek Dr., (800) 991-2338, columbiagorge.org*

Fort Dalles Historical Museum ___139

📍 ***Location:*** The Dalles, OR
🕐 ***Hours:*** Closed in winter limited hours

Built in 1850, Fort Dalles was the only fort between Wyoming and the Pacific Coast. It was constructed to protect the pioneers making their way west and to serve as a logistics depot for military supplies. Today, the U.S. Army Surgeon's Headquarters is the only remaining structure and is now a small museum full of local pioneer artifacts. Outside, there's a barn with antique cars, buggies and surries. Kids can ring the big bells on the cars. Make sure to call before you go as the museum is open at various times. Combine this with a visit to Sorosis Park, just up the hill, and you'll have a great afternoon. Admission is $3 for adults; 18 and under free.

🚗 **Getting There:** From Hood River, drive 20 miles east on I-84 to Exit 83 (W. 6th St.). Turn left onto 6th St., right onto Trevitt St. then left on W. 15th St. until Garrison St. *W. 15th St. and Garrison St., (541) 296-4547, www.historicthedalles.org*

Gorge Heritage Museum _____ 140

☛ **Location:** Bingen, WA
🛇 **Hours:** Closed in winter, limited hours

For hands-on lessons about pioneers and people from Klickitat and Skamania Counties, pop into the museum and play at their mock country store, stocked with butter paddles and milk jars.

🚣 **Getting There:** Cross the Hood River Birdge, turn right on Hwy. 14, and make a left on Maple St. *202 E. Humboldt St., , (509) 493-3228, community.gorge.net/ghmuseum*

History Museum of Hood River_____141

☛ **Location:** Hood River, OR
🛇 **Hours:** Closed in winter, limited hours

Tucked away near the Marina, this museum has interesting artifacts from Hood River's past, including Native American beaded bags and a 100-year-old slice of wedding cake. The museum is very Hood River Valley-specific. They have traveling exhibits to keep you coming back and big plans for the future! Donations encouraged and the docents (all volunteers) take time to answer questions. If you call in advance, the docents will have games, even a scavenger hunt, to keep your little one curious about our town's history.

🚣 **Getting There:** From I-84 go north at Exit 64. At the stop sign turn left and follow the signs to the museum. 300 E. Port Marina Dr., *(541) 386-6772, www.co.hood-river.or.us/museum*

Hutson Museum _____142

☛ **Location:** Parkdale, OR
🛇 **Hours:** Closed in winter, train hours.

This museum boasts a unique rock collection which looks likes a delicious meal. Don't eat it or you'll head straight to the dentist! The museum's hours coincide with the Mt. Hood Railroad train. If you are in Parkdale when the train's there or if you're on the train, this is a good quick stop. Admission: $1 for adults; $.50 for older kids.

🚣 **Getting There:** Drive south on Hwy. 35 for 13 miles toward Parkdale. Turn right onto Cooper Spur Rd. at the Mt. Hood Country Store. Drive another two miles and turn right on Baseline Dr. *4967 Baseline Dr.(541) 352-6808*

Maryhill Museum _____143

🢒 **Location:** *Maryhill, WA*
🥄 **Hours:** *Mid-March-mid-November, daily 10:00 am to 4:30 pm*

Now, what in Sam Hill is a museum doing in the middle of nowhere? The castle-like mansion was built in 1914 by Sam Hill, a wealthy entrepreneur and attorney who was also instrumental in building the Old Columbia River Highway. Sam Hill built the mansion to lure his wife, Mary, to the area. She never came and the home eventually became a museum. The museum has a superb collection of chess sets and one of the largest displays of France's Auguste Rodin sculptures outside of Paris. There's a small café inside or you can picnic outside in the garden full of sculptures and meandering peacocks. Don't bring your diaper bags and backpacks inside (not allowed!). Admission: $7 for adults; $2 for children 6-16.

🚗 **Getting There:** Take I-84 east 40 miles to Exit 104. Drive across the Sam Hill Bridge into Washington and head north on Hwy. 97 until you reach Hwy. 14. Go west 3 miles. *35 Maryhill Museum Dr., (509) 773-3733, www.maryhillmuseum.org*

WAAAM Museum _____144

🢒 **Location:** *Hood River, OR*
🥄 **Hours:** *9:00 to 5:00 pm*

This Western Antique Aeroplane and Automobile Museum (WAAAM) contains one of the nations largest collections of flying antique aero planes. What's even more amazing is that all the planes in the hangar fly. Director of the museum, Jeremy Young, says that he wouldn't have it otherwise -- "that would be like going to the zoo and seeing stuffed animals." They also have a fleet of old cars taking you back in time. My favorite is the T Tour Car, the same model as the one in Chitty Chitty Bang Bang. Although most of the exhibits are for looking only, they plan on adding a few cars and planes that your little one can sit on. Time your visit with one of their special events, and you'll see their old planes flying overhead. Admission: $8 for adults; $6 for children 5-18; and $2 for children under two.

🚗 **Getting There:** Head south on 13th Street to Tucker Road. Look for the airport and museum on your left. 1600 Air Museum Rd.., (541) 308-1600, www.waaamuseum.org

Playgroups/Areas

New Parent Services Playgroup ___ 145

☞ **Location:** *Hood River, OR*

Looking for a group of parents with kids the same age as yours? New Parent Services sponsors several playgroups, which meet every Thursday and Friday in the Riverside Community Church downtown. It is free; all parents and caretakers are welcome.

🚶 **Getting There:** The Riverside Community Church is near downtown Hood River on 4th St. and State St. For up to date information, check *www.gorgekids.com and www.community.gorge.net/nextdoor*

Our Children's Place _____ 146

☞ **Location:** *Hood River, OR*

Owner Teacher Janet has a wealth of experience to share with your kids. Our Children's Place is a preschool, plus it offer lots of special classes over the year. The drop-in play area is designed for parents to come and play with their kids or simply hang-out with other parents.

🚶 **Getting There:** Drive up 12th Street and Our Children's Place is on the left. *1110 12th St., (541) 386-1975, www.TeacherJanet.com*

Play at Wonderworks _____ 147

☞ **Location:** *The Dalles, OR*

Photo by Jenny Loughmiller

If your kids are going stir crazy, head east to Wonderworks Playstation for some indoor fun. Wonderworks is a volunteer-run, non-profit organization geared for young children. The indoor community playroom is equipped with art supplies, tumbling mats, play kitchens and other fun toys. Activities cater to young children four and under, but six year olds also have fun. They offer music, cooking, parenting and other classes. The group has plans to evolve into a much larger Children's Museum with traveling exhibits for kids of all ages. Daily admission $3 for the first child, $1 additional child or yearly membership of $25 per family.

Getting There: Head east on I-84 for 19.8 miles to Exit 84. Take a right on Union St. and a left on 5th St, 111 East 5th St., *(541) 298-7268, www.wonderworktd.org*

Kid Classes

Community Education _____ 148

Pick up a schedule of classes at the Hood River Public Library or go by the Community Education Office. There are tons of great classes for kids from circus camps, to soccer, art, cooking and more.

Getting There: Community Education Office is in the Coe Primary Building. *1009 Eugene St., Hood River, (541) 386-2055, www.hrcommunityed.org*

Dance Classes _____ 149

The Columbia Gorge Dance Academy offers ballet, jazz, tap, hip hop classes and a special "Mom, Dad and Me" class for toddlers. Classes are usually held during the school year from September to June, but they also have some summer classes.

Summer dressed for recital

Photo by Clint Bogard

Getting There: In Hood River, drive south on 13th St. Turn right on May St. *2600 May Avenue, Hood River, (541) 386-6044, www.columbiagorgedanceacademy.com*

Eclipse Music Center_____152

This music center offers both private and group classes ranging from classic piano and violin to a rock and roll band. A variety of teachers and lots of classes to choose from.

Getting There: Downtown Hood River on the corner of 4th and State Sts., *212 4th St., (541) 386-3681, www.musiceclipse.com*

Gymnastics _____ 150

Let your kids channel their energy towards working on balance, coordination and strength in a gymnastics class at the Hood River Sports Club. Parents join their toddlers in their first class.

Getting There: Head south on 13th St. and make a right on Brookside Rd. at the traffic light to the club. *1330 Brookside Rd., Hood River, (541) 386-3230, www.hrsportsclub.com*

Tae Kwan Do _____151

The Northwest Tae Kwan Do Center teaches kids the Korean martial art of Tae Kwan Do, loosely translated to "foot and hand way." Students learn the special kicks and some can even break wood with their bare hands. Classes are held during the year.

Bryce testing for his next belt

Photo by Kevin Donald www.columbiagorgeimages.com

Getting There: From downtown Hood River, drive up 13th St., make a left on B St. and a left on 12th St. The studio is in the back. *1203 12th St., Hood River, (541) 387-3222*

Flow Yoga Studio _____ 151

Yoga is a super way for kids to learn about their bodies and their calmer selves. While your children are doing their downward facing dogs, you can practice the Eagle Pose in a separate class. Decadent? The folks at Flow know how to make you feel good.

Audrey doing her downward facing dog

Photo by Ruth

🚶 **Getting There:** Downtown Hood River on 3rd St., between Oak and Cascade. *118 3rd St., (541) FUN-Yoga, www.hoodriverflow.com*

Other Indoor Activities

Paint a Pot: Ceramics _____ 154

☞ *Location:* Hood River, OR

Working with clay is an excellent creative project for a rainy day. You may become a regular customer like many kids around town. The

Jason painting his train

Photo by Jody

KV Ceramic Studio is equipped with all sorts of pottery -- be it animals, plates, mugs or trains -- that your kids can paint and glaze. Try making a handprint for Grandma. This is one of the few drop-in art places around town, so it's a hit.

🚶 **Getting There:** Head south on 13th St. until it turns into Tucker Rd. The KV Ceramic Studio is on the right just before Good News Gardening. *1082 Tucker Rd., (541) 386-4664*

Go Bowling _____ 153

☞ **Location:** *Hood River, OR*
🕯 **Hours:** *Open daily*

Orchard Lanes has 16 lanes,
some which are geared for
the novice bowler because
the gutters can be blocked.
They offer a youth rate for
kids 17 and under. $1.75 a
game.

Photo by Robin Dickinson

Poised to strike!

🛶 **Getting There:** From Oak St., turn south on 13th St. which
turns into Tucker Rd. The bowling alley is on the left. *1141 Tucker
Rd., (541) 386-1326 www.orchardlanes.net*

Make a Glass Tile _____ 155

☞ **Location:** *White Salmon, WA*
🕯 **Hours:** *Closed Mondays*

White Salmon Glassworks offers classes and workshops on glass blowing, glass fusing and bead making. You can design your own glass tile
and in November and December you can blow your own ornament.
A perfect gift! The hot fire requires extreme caution, especially with
little ones.

🛶 **Getting There:** Cross the Hood River Bridge, turn right on
Hwy. 14. Drive through Bingen and turn left on Hwy. 141/ E.
Jewett Blvd. until you reach the main street. 105 E. Jewett Blvd.,
(509) 493-8400, www.whitesalmonglassworks.com

Go to the Movies! _____ 156

- **Cascade Cinema:** *1410 W. 6th, The Dalles, (541) 298-2600, www
  .moviesinthedalles.com*
- **Columbia Cinema:** *2727 W. 7th St., The Dalles, (541) 296-8081,
  www.moviesinthedalles.com*
- **Hood River Cinema:** *5 5th Street, Hood River, (541) 386-7503,
  www.hoodrivercinemas.com*
- **Skylight Theatre:** equipped with couches, serves pizza and is
  adult-only after 8:00 pm. *107 Oak St., Hood River, (541) 386-
  4888, www.skylighttheatre.com*

Chapter 14

We All Scream for Ice Cream

Your kids will probably place this category on the top of your "to do" list. Sometimes our children even scream for ice cream before breakfast. Yes, for some of us, ice cream is a necessity in life. If not an outing on its own, ice cream stops go hand-in-hand with a waterfall hike or an escape from one of our hot summer days. Here's the scoop.

Luke really enjoying his ice cream

Photo by Kelly Brown

Alabama Jim's * Apple Valley Country Store * Doppio * Eastwind Drive-In * Grounds * Jonny's Ice Cream & Deli * Mike's Ice Cream * Route 30 Classics and Roadside Refreshments

Alabama Jim's ———————— 163

☞ **Location:** *Parkdale, OR*
🍴 **Season:** *Open daily all year*

Named for the owner's father, who worked as a chef for general's in the military, Alabama Jim's is a classic ice cream store. They serve both Umpqua and Tillamook ice cream. Try their licorice ice cream, and your tongue may never be the same. Just take a look at the dramatic pictures posted inside! This hang-out also serves sandwiches, soups and other lunch food. If you are in Parkdale looking for a treat, look no further! Kids scoops are only $1.00

Connor loves strawberry ice cream

Black tongue disease

🚶 **Getting There:** From I-84, take Exit 64 south, drive 13 miles on Hwy. 35. Turn right onto Cooper Spur Rd. at the Mt. Hood Country Store. Go another two miles and turn right on Baseline Dr. into town. *4946 Baseline Dr., (541) 352-3553*

Apple Valley Country Store ———— 157

☞ **Location:** *Hood River, OR*
🍴 **Season:** *Closed in winter, varied hours in Summer*

This country classic situated right at the Hood River's bend has the best fruit shakes around made with real fruit! Choose from huckleberry, marionberry, strawberry and more! If you're not in the mood for a shake, sample their jams, jellies and mustards or eat apple pie. They have an outdoor BBQ in the summer. Kids love watching the goats. Although they can't get inside the goat pen, kids can experience the goats' "tickle tongues" as they nibble the pellets.

🚶 **Getting There:** From Cascade Ave. turn right on 13th St. Drive 5 miles south on 12th St., which becomes Tucker Rd. *2363 Tucker Rd., (541) 386-1971, www.applevaleystore.com*

Doppio _____ 158

🐾 **Location:** *Hood River, OR*
▌ **Season:** *Open year round*

This more upscale coffee/ lunch/ ice cream place serves home-made gelato ice cream, frozen yogurt and healthy smoothies. Families enjoy savoring their ice cream on the steps outside while playing around the fountain.

🚶 **Getting There:** On the main drag between 3rd and 4th. *310 Oak St, (541) 386-3000, www.doppiocafe.com*

Eastwind Drive In _____ 158

🐾 **Location:** *Cascade Locks, OR*
▌ **Season:** *Open year round*

If you're looking to cool off with a melt-in-the-mouth soft ice cream, then this is the place for you. Some rave that its better than Dairy Queen. They also serve fastfood burgers and fries. Dessert first?

🚶 **Getting There:** From Hood River, drive 16 miles west on I-84 to Exit 44, Cascade Locks. Drive one mile into town and the Drive-In is on the right side. *395 Wa-Na-Pa Street, (541) 374-8380*

Grounds _____ 160

🐾 **Location:** *White Salmon, WA*
▌ **Season:** *Open year round*

Since The Creamery closed down, Grounds is now the local place to hang-out, drink coffee and eat ice cream. The Rainbow Sherbet is the best seller, but don't forget about the rootbeer floats and banana splits made with Cascade Glacier ice cream. Partner this with a trip to the White Salmon library or a park for a perfect outing.

🚶 **Getting There:** Cross the Hood River Bridge, turn left on Hwy. 14. and a quick right onto Dock Grade Rd. Head up the hill and turn left on Jewett Blvd. Grounds is on the north side of the main street. *166 E. Jewett Blvd., (509) 493-1340*

Johnny's Ice Cream and Deli _____ 159

 Location: *Cascade Locks, OR*
Season: *Open year round*

According to one of the grandmothers in the bunch, this ice cream store serves the best ice cream east of Portland. They also sell soups and sandwiches. If your kids aren't tall enough to shoot some pool, you can savor your ice cream on their outside patio.

Getting There: From I-84 in Hood River, drive 16 miles west to Exit 44 in Cascade Locks. Drive one mile on Wa-Na-Pa St. The ice cream store is on the left side nestled next to the courthouse. *424 SW Wa-Na-Pa Street, (541) 374-8300*

Mike's Ice Cream _____ 161

Location: *Hood River, OR*
Season: *Closed in Winter*

Our kids vote Mike's the best place to eat ice cream in the Gorge. On a hot day, a visit to Mike's is a must and you'll probably find plenty of other families enjoying their cones. They serve Prince Pucklers' ice cream made in Eugene. The location of this adorable ice cream shack and the atmosphere will make you want to come back again and again. An added bonus is the climbing tree growing to the left of the store. While you're eating your scoop, check out the bulletin board to find out what's happening in town.

Getting There: Mike's is on the main street of Hood River across from the library. *504 Oak St., (541) 386-6260*

Rutger and Sawyer seriously evaluating their ice cream

Photo by Clint Bogard

Route 30 Classics and Roadside Refreshments _____ 162

🐾 **Location:** *Mosier, OR*
❚ **Season:** *Closed in winter*

This ice cream store is one of a kind. What other ice cream store cohabitates with a Porsche dealership? You can enjoy your ice cream sitting on the high bar stools along the window overlooking the main road of the sleepy town of Mosier. If you have enough money in the piggy jar, you may leave with a satisfied sweet tooth and a fancy sports car. The Umpqua ice cream is tasty and the store is cool.

Kids screaming for ice cream --
next comes the Porsche!

🏊 **Getting There:** From I-84 in Hood River, drive east to Exit 69. Make a right at the end of the off-ramp and follow Rt. 30. *1100 1st Ave., Mosier, (541) 478-2525*

Happenings Around the Hood

Rich with community events, here in the Gorge almost every week-end in the summer there's something interesting going on. Maybe it's music in the park, a festival, or the County Fair. What follows isn't an exhaustive list, but rather festivities that the whole family will enjoy.

Mindy smiling in the cherry blossoms

Photo by Susan Harkness

First Fridays * Kids Carnival * Blossom Festival * Earth Day * Cherry Festival * Saturday Market * Spring Fest * Cycling Classic * Fiddle Contest * Fishing * Horse Show * Dance Recital * Thomas the Tank Engine * Fourth of July * Rodeo * Gorge Games * County Fair * Concert in the Park * Fly-In * Huckleberry Festival * Soap Box Derby * Festival of Nations * Harvest Festival * Halloween * The Nutcracker

March

First Fridays _____ 164

☞ **Location:** *Hood River, OR*
🕯 **When:** *First Friday of the month from March-December*

On the first Friday beginning at 5:00 pm of every month from March until December, local artists team up with downtown stores to exhibit their masterpieces. Many stores serve food and wine and stay open until 8:00 pm. Musicians play on every block. Sometimes the street is closed to car traffic. Bring your family, stroll the street and bump into all your friends. One of the First Fridays features an outdoor chalk drawing contest, which our kids love. There's always something fun for kids.

Photo by Susan Shepherd

Taylor pedaling ice cream at First Friday

🚶 **Getting There:** Oak St. in downtown Hood River.

Mt. Hood Meadows Kids Carnival __165

☞ **Location:** *Mt. Hood, OR*
🕯 **When:** *Mid-March*

Our local ski resort hosts a snow carnival geared for kids from 4 to 12 years old. There's a huge ice castle with a slide that kids can climb on and sled down, an obstacle course, races, and live music.

🚶 **Getting There:** From I-84 in Hood River, go south at Exit 64. Drive 36 miles on Hwy. 35 until you see the signs for Mt. Hood Meadows. There are two parking lots. If your kids are just learning to ski, park in the top lot where the lodge and fun zone are accessible. *(800) SKI-HOOD, www.skihood.com*

April

Hood River Valley Blossom Festival_166

🐾 *Location:* Hood River Valley, OR
❙ *When:* Third weekend in April

When the blossoms are out, thousands of people flock to the Hood River Valley to celebrate their arrival. The festival takes place all over the valley and features art and music, antique, quilt and craft shows, and tours of the orchards. Kids love running around in the orchards -- especially when the apple, pear and cherry trees look they are covered with white and pink popcorn. Hood River Fruit Loop, *(800) 366-3530, www.hoodriverfruitloop and www.hoodriver.org*

Earth Day _____ 167

🐾 *Location:* Hood River, OR
❙ *When:* middle of April

Earth Day is a big deal in the Gorge because we love our earth and want to combat global warming. Celebrations include a run/walk on the Old Highway, costume-making sessions, and a Procession of Species parade. Watch out for the salmon! Remember to recycle and re-use. Columbia Gorge Earth Center, (541) 387-0063, www.cgec.org

Photo by Ruth

Is that a salmon on the street?

The Dalles Cherry Festival _____ 168

🐾 *Location:* The Dalles, OR
❙ *When:* Third weekend in April

The Dalles brings on the blossoms with lots of festivities, including a parade, food contest, dance party, bike ride and much more. Its a festive welcome and lots of fun activities for kids. (800) 255-3385, *www.thedalleschamber.com/cherryfestival.htm*

May

Hood River's Saturday Market____169

☞ **Location:** Hood River, OR
🕐 **When:** Saturday 9:00 to 3:00 pm from May-October

Every Saturday morning, farmers bring their produce and artists show their wares at the market. The market often hosts kid-related activities such as dog costume contests, children's art, music and more. It's a good place to stroll, buy local fruit, dig into a warm bag of kettle corn, dance to the live music, savor a tamale, eat kettle corn, meet all your friends, and munch on kettle corn. Did we mention the kettle corn? The market takes place in the parking lot at the corner Cascade Ave. and 5th St. *(541) 387-8349*

Learning to raise funds
at Saturday Market

Photo by Lorraine Carlstrom

White Salmon Spring Fest_____170

☞ **Location:** White Salmon, WA
🕐 **When:** End of May

This three-day festival gives a small town welcome to the spring flowers and warm weather. Kids dress up for the parade, get their face painted, laugh with the clowns and dance to music. *(509) 365-4565, www.whitesalmonspringfestival.com*

Mt. Hood Cycling Classic _____ 171

▌ When: *End of May*

This week-long bike race brings the professional cyclists to the Gorge. For the women, the 2008 competition was an Olympic qualifying event. There's a fun kid's race and the town loves to cheer the racers especially at the criterium. *www.mthoodcyclingclassic.com*

Sizing up the competition

Columbia Gorge Fiddle Contest ___ 172

☛ Location: *Hood River, OR*
▌ When: *Beginning of May*

Fiddlers from all over convene in Hood River to play their tunes. We have some amazing talent in our own backyard, including Hood River native and Oregon champion, Matthew McCravey. You may even find fiddlers on the roof. *www.columbiagorgefiddlecontest.com*

Youth Fishing Clinic at the Laurance Lake Ponds _____173

☛ Location: *Parkdale, OR*
▌ When: *Mid-May*

This clinic is a perfect first fishing experience. The Forest Service hands out fishing poles and bait to kids 13 years and younger. They also paint faces, cook hot dogs and hold fishing contests.

🚶 Getting There: Take I-84 to Exit 64. Drive 12 miles south on Hwy. 35. Turn right at the Mt. Hood Country Store and follow signs to Parkdale. In Parkdale, make a left on Clear Creek Rd. Drive 3 miles and turn right at the Laurance Lake sign. The pond is 2 miles up the road. *(541) 352-6002, www.fs.fed.us*

June

Passport to Fishing Day at Bonneville Fish Hatchery_____174

🐟 **Location:** *Bonneville Dam, OR*
🕐 **When:** *Early June*

Ready to catch the big one? The Bonneville Fish Hatchery opens its waters to kids 12 and under. You don't have to bring a thing ... for fishing, that is. Kids are given loaner fishing poles, and there's plenty of fish to catch and other fish-oriented activities.

🚶 **Getting There:** From I-84 in Hood River drive west 22 miles to Exit 40. Turn right and follow the signs. Bonneville Fish Hatchery, *(541) 374-8820 www.nwp.usace.army.mil*

Hood River Classic Horse Show ___175

🐟 **Location:** *Hood River, OR*
🕐 **When:** *Mid-June*

This hunter/jumper horse show attracts top-notch riders from the Northwest and beyond. If your kids have any interest in horses, then you have to attend and watch riders demonstrate their skills. We love meandering the grounds and looking at the beautiful horses. Wear your sun hat because after all this is a horse event, plus shade can be hard to find.

Tally ho!

Photo by Cloud 9

🚶 **Getting There:** From I-84 go south at Exit 64. Drive 12 miles on Hwy. 35, turn right on Leisure Rd. and you'll see Jensen Mills Meadows. *(541) 354-2009, www.hoodriverclassic.com*

Dance Academy's Spring Recital__176

☞ **Location:** *Hood River, OR*
🕯 **When:** *Mid-June*

The Columbia Gorge Dance Academy puts on an impressive spring recital where students perform ballet, tap, hip hop and jazz. For a small town, we have lots of talent and very supportive families. The performance usually happens at the Hood River Middle School on May St. (541) 386-3267, www.columbiagorgedanceacademy.com

Thomas the Tank Engine _____177

☞ **Location:** *Hood River, OR*
🕯 **When:** *Late June*

Thomas toots his whistle in the Hood. For those Thomas fans, this is the major event of the summer. Even Sir Topham Hat shows up. The train ride that leaves from the Mt. Hood Railroad station in Hood River is about 30 minutes long, a perfect amount of time. Tickets are $14 for everyone 1 and up.

🛶 **Getting There:** Mt. Hood Railroad is on the left at the end of Cascade Ave. *110 Railroad Ave., (800) 872-4661, www.mthoodrr.com*

July

Fourth of July in Hood River__178

☞ **Location:** *Hood River, OR*
🕯 **When:** *4th of July*

Get an old car, unicycle or fire truck, and enter the parade! This small town celebration weaves down 13th Street and ends with music, hot dogs and apple pie at Jackson Park. If you don't want to be in the parade, you can watch from the sidelines while your kids scramble after candy thrown from the floats. Wear your red, white, and blue!

Our town parade

Courtesy of Hood River News

Fort Dalles Pro Rodeo _____ 179

☞ **Location:** *The Dalles, OR*
🕮 **When:** *Mid-July*

Cowgirls, cowboys, wild broncos and bulls -- the rodeo is full of dust, music, food, dancing, tournaments, parades and even a queen who oversees the crowd. Come see the pros rope the calves and ride the bulls -- just don't try it yourself! Tickets are $10-$13; if you go on Thursday's Family Night, then the whole family gets in for $25.

🛶 **Getting There:** From I-84, go east 20 miles to The Dalles. Take the 6th St. exit, make a left at W. 6th St. Turn left on Webber St. which becomes River Rd. *2652 River Rd., (800) 255-3385, www.fortdallesrodeo.com*

Gorge Games _____ 180

☞ **Location:** *All over the Gorge, (Hood River headquarters)*
🕮 **When:** *Third week in July*

The Gorge Games brings a host of out-door athletic competitions, including skateboarding, riverboarding, kiteboarding, cycling and adventure racing. Its one of the premier outdoor sporting events in the Pacific Northwest and there's lots of fun events for kids (and adults) to watch, volunteer and even participate.. The Games sponsors a number of clinics/classes for kids, including sailing, rock climbing, kayaking, BMX skills and much more. *www.gorgegames.net*

A Sky high invert

Photo by Pam Miller

☺ Hood River County Fair_____ 181

☞ **Location:** *Hood River, OR*
🕮 **When:** *End of-July*

We look forward to this event because of the animals and the rides. The 4H kids show their horses, pigs, chickens, bulls, guinea pigs, sheep, rabbits, geese, and more. The amusement rides range from gentle to the fast-spinning-hold-on-to-your stomach experience.

Getting There:
From downtown Hood River, drive up 13th until it turns into Tucker Rd., turn left at the Odell Hwy. and right on Wy'East Rd. *3020 Wy'east Rd., Hood River, (541) 354-2865, www.hoodriverfair.com*

Photo by Susan Lucas

The rides at the County Fair

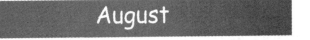

August

😊Families in the Park Concert Series_182

Location: *Hood River, OR*
When: *7:00 pm every Thursday in August*

Every Thursday night in August, it seems like all of Hood River gathers for a concert at Jackson Park. Families picnic, listen to music and dance. Food vendors open at 6:00 pm and music starts at 7:00 pm. Get there early to stake out a plot of grass as the park fills up fast. Bring lawn chairs, bug spray and a picnic.

Getting There: From I-84 go south at Exit 62. Take Cascade Ave. to 13th St. and turn right up the hill. Jackson Park is at the corner of 13th St. and May St. *(541) 386-2055*

Hood River Fly-In_____183

Location: *Hood River, OR*
When: *End of August*

For kids and adults that love planes, this event is not to be missed. The Fly-In celebrates the bird's eye view of our surroundings. The airport and our new WAAM Museum hosts all sorts of planes, from model airplanes to gliders to biplanes. The location of the Fly-In alternates yearly between Hood River and The Dalles.

Getting There: From I-84 go south at Exit 62. Take Cascade Ave. to 13th St., which turns into Tucker Rd. Turn left onto Airport Dr. *(541) 386-1133, www.flythegorge.com*

September

Huckleberry Festival _____184

☞ *Location:* Bingen, WA
☗ *When:* Early September

The City of Bingen kicks off this festival with a small town parade featuring fire trucks, old cars, politicians and floats. Everyone ends up at the park for food, music and carnival rides.

Getting There: Cross the Hood River Toll Bridge and turn right onto Hwy. 14. Drive one mile and turn left on Willow St. You'll see the sign for "City Park". *City of Bingen, (509) 493-2122*

Hood River Soap Box Derby_____185

☞ *Location:* Hood River, OR
☗ *When:* All-day usually the third Saturday in September

The Derby is a competition for children 8 to 16 years old. They hop in their home-made soap boxes and race down the hill. Building the cars is half the fun -- many kids use kits purchased from the All-American Soap Box Association.

Getting There: Wasco St. Call for exact location. *Columbia River Soap Box Derby, (541) 386-4950, www.crsbd.com*

Festival of Nations _____186

☞ *Location:* Cascade Locks, OR
☗ *When:* end of September

Together with the Warm Springs Tribe, the city of Cascade Locks opens up the Marina Park to ethnic dancers, food, music and games for the kids. There's even a run for the athletic souls and some great dancing and drumming. *www.festivalofnations.info*

October

Hood River Valley Harvest Festival_187

☞ **Location:** *Hood River Valley, OR*
🏮 **When:** *Third weekend in October*

This popular festival celebrates apples, pears, pumpkins, and the fall. Down at the Expo Center, you'll find artisans, musicians and delicious food. At the Fairgrounds in Odell, you can buy fruit and vegetables from the local farmers. In Parkdale, you'll find a market with artists, bands, and food. Grab a Fruit Loop map and travel from farm to farm. Some of the fun stops for children are: Rasmussen Farms' corn field maze, the Alpaca farm, and Kiyokawa Orchard's hay rides.

🚶 **Getting There:** Start at the Expo Center or your closest orchard and navigate your way through the Hood River Valley. *(800) 366-3530, www.hoodriver.org*

Halloween _____ 188

There's so much going on for Halloween that you might want to have a variety of Halloween costumes. Here's what we like to do:

Meadows Mtn. View Farms _____ 189

☞ **Location:** *White Salmon, WA*

Known for its peaches, this family farm celebrates Halloween in style. People ride to the pumpkin fields in the farm's tractor and the horse-pulled wagon. There are also plenty of goats, pigs, sheep and donkeys to feed.

🚶 **Getting There:** Cross the Hood River Bridge and turn left on Hwy. 14. Turn right on Hwy. 141 Alt. Turn right two miles up onto Arnett Rd. *#8 The Knoll, White Salmon, (509) 493-2358*

Can she carry this one?

Parkdale Pumpkin Parade _____ 190

☞ **Location:** *Parkdale, OR*

Put on a costume and enter this small community parade. Create a float, decorate a stroller or a bike and join the parade!

🚗 **Getting There:** From I-84, take Exit 64 south to Hwy. 35. Go 13 miles and turn right onto Cooper Spur Rd. The parade starts across from the fire station. *(541) 352-6280*

Rasmussen Farms _____ 191

☞ **Location:** *Hood River, OR*

A pumpkin patch and much, much more! Don't miss the cornfield maze, the pumpkin head decorations, popcorn, fresh apples and pears. Warning: your kids may make you return more than once!

🚗 **Getting There:** Go south at Exit 64 and drive 5.5 miles on Hwy. 35. Make a left on Fir Mtn. Rd. and a right on Thomsen Rd. *3020 Thomsen Rd., (541) 386-4622, www.rasmussenfarms.com*

Trick or Treating _____ 192

☞ **Location:** *Hood River, OR*

Downtown Hood River is a popular place to trick or treat. The stores open their doors and hand out tricks and treats. Some businesses even set up haunted houses with ghosts, goblins and witches. The homes on Cascade near downtown also go wild with decorations. Consider a Halloween fairy who takes the bounty in exchange for a wish. Better for teeth.

What a cute little pair of bugs

Photo by Ruth

December

The Nutcracker _____ 193

☞ *Location: Hood River, OR*

Thanks to Nancy Clement, a former professional dancer and current owner and teacher at the Dance Academy, the Nutcracker performance is a must-see. Costumes are first class and the smiles on the dancers as they pirouette around the stage make every parent proud. Performances are usually at the Hood River Middle School.

Photo by Jim Semlor

The Dew Drop Fairies

Columbia Gorge Hotel Lights _____ 194

☞ *Location: Hood River, OR*

In true Christmas spirit, the grand Columbia Gorge Hotel lights their gardens with thousands of white lights. We love to stroll their grounds and marvel at their 200 foot waterfall, that plunges down to the river.

🛶 **Getting There:** From I-84 take Exit 62 north and turn left on Westcliff Dr. *(800) 345-1921, www.columbiagorgehotel.com*

Other Holiday Events
- **Hood River Hotel:** Don't miss their festive tree decorating evening featuring music, carolers and the man with the beard.
- **Skamania Lodge:** Decorate a gingerbread house and learn from the chefs who make a intricate gingerbread village.

Chapter 16

Childcare and Babysitting

As every parent knows, one of our biggest challenges is finding good help. When choosing a babysitter or daycare center, make sure to thoroughly check out the person or place before leaving your child.

Bambino's Learning Center_____195

This bilingual facility located in both White Salmon and Hood River offers drop-in care, classes and activities for infants to school aged children. The center also has a nanny and babysitter referral service and they're open late on weekends. 2020 Clearwater Lane, Hood River (541) 386-2005; 871 NE Estes, White Salmon, *(509) 493-8525, www.bambinoslearningcenter.com*

Child Care Partners_____196

Funded in part by the government, this service helps working families in Hood River and Wasco County find appropriate childcare. 400 E. Scenic Dr., The Dalles, *(800) 755-1143*

🙂 Gorgekids.com Website_____197

This valuable website not only offers information about events and activities for families in the Gorge, but it also has a section for finding babysitters and daycare providers. *www.gorgekids.com*

Gorge.net Website_____198

Gorge.net's classified section is an excellent way to search for babysitters. You can also look for other things you may need. Post your request in the "help wanted" section. *www.gorge.net*

Photo by David Maccabee

Chapter 17

Kid-Friendly Restaurants

Would you like to go out to eat where you can get a highchair, paper and crayons, maybe some toys or enough background noise that no one is bothered by your children? Here are some of the restaurants in and around the Gorge where you won't have to cringe when you walk in with the whole brood. Bon Appetit!

Outdoor dining at Three Rivers Grill

Photo by Tim

Breakfast Places * Coffeehouses * Dinner/ Lunch Spots * Food to Go * Outdoor Seating * Playground Restaurants * Quick Bites

What is a kid-friendly restaurant?

It is a restaurant that has made a concerted effort to cater to families because they recognize the challenge of eating out with small children. For the most part, almost all of the restaurants in the Gorge are kid-friendly. We categorized the list into coffeehouses, breakfast places, dinner spots, outdoor seating, playground restaurants, quick bites and food to go. We thought this highlighted each restaurant's best quality in terms of kid-friendliness. If you want to bring the family to some of the finer establishments, we suggest going early and not on a weekend.

Breakfast Places_____ 201

- **Best Western Hood River Inn:** Consider Sunday brunch on their deck overlooking the river. 1108 East Marina Way, *Hood River, (541) 386-2200, www.hoodriverinn.com*
- **Bette's Place:** A classic breakfast place with hometown cooking and infamous cinnamon buns. They love kids and don't cry over spilled milk. *416 Oak St., (541) 386-1880, www.bettesplace.com*
- **Egg Harbor Cafe :** Serves a hearty breakfast in booths where kids can hide away. *1313 Oak Street, Hood River, (541) 386-1127*
- **Sage's Cafe:** Breakfast on blueberry pancakes and apple dumplings to write home about. Big tables and plenty of space. 202 *Oak Street, Hood River, (541) 386-9404, www.sagescafe.biz*
- **Hood River Hotel:** Our local hotel on the main street has fine dining. For brunch, you can eat pancakes made with organic eggs outside on the deck or play with the toys in the lobby. *102 Oak Avenue, Hood River, (541) 386-1900, www.hoodriverhotel.com*
- **Windseeker:** This restaurant has a 1950s feel. The Belgian waffles combined with the river view and garden with carp in the ponds makes for a great breakfast. *1535 Bargeway Rd., The Dalles, (541) 298-7171, www.windseekerrestaurant.com*

Coffeehouses_____ 200

- **10-Speed Coffee:** Cool bicycle chairs and a space upstairs where kids can play freely. The new digs in Mosier have outside tables. *1412 13th St., Hood River, (541) 386-3165, 1104 Hwy. 30, Mosier, www.10speedcoffee.com*
- **Acres Organic Coffee House:** Drive through or eat/drink in. They have great baked goods and healthy soups. *1235 State St., Hood River, (541) 387-2273*

- **Bahma Coffee Bar:** Bahma in Hebrew means "one's place of personal comfort." This local hot spot lives up to its name. 77 Russell Ave., Stevenson, *(509) 427-8700, www.bahmacoffeebar.com*
- **Dog River:** This popular coffee hang-out has comfortable couches in the back and games and toys for kids. 411 Oak St., *Hood River, (541) 386-4502, www.dogrivercoffee.com*
- **Espresso Your Love:** Good coffee, delicious baked goods and lots of space to play. *3400 Odell Hwy., Odell, (541) 354-3400*
- **Good News Gardening:** Their garden cafe feels like you're in an elegant living room with tasty organic food. 1086 Tucker Rd., *Hood River, (541) 386-6438, www.goodnewsgardening.com*
- **Grounds Cafe:** The White Salmon cafe may lure more families, but both work well for a quick cup of jo, even ice cream or a hot chocolate. *12 Oak Street, Hood River, (541) 386-4442; 166 E. Jewett Blvd., White Salmon, (509) 493-1340*
- **Holstein's Coffee:** Kids dig the smoothies and playing board games in the cafe. *811 E. 3rd St., The Dalles, (541) 298-2326.*

Dinner/ Lunch Spots _____ 202

- **Big River Grill:** Classic burgers and lots of historical photos and other interesting things to gaze at inside. *192 SW 2nd St., Stevenson, (509) 427-4888, www.bigrivergrill.us*
- **Casa El Mirador:** Delicious Mexican food and quick service. *302 W. 2nd St., The Dalles, (541) 298-7388, www.casaelmirador.com*
- **China Gorge:** Our kids love the General Tsao's chicken. The noodles and potstickers are also a hit. *2680 Old Columbia River Hwy., Hood River, (541) 386-5331, www.chinagorge.com*
- **Cousins Restaurant:** This diner-style restaurant has a miniature train and farm animals that don't have to be fed. *2114 W. 6th Street, The Dalles, (541) 298-2771, www.cousinsinthedalles.com*
- **Crazy Pepper Cantina:** Once you enter this Mexican restaurant, crayons and chips and salsa will be at your table. *103 4th Street, Hood River, (541) 387-2454*
- **El Tapatio :** A Mexican restaurant in the Heights with big portions, comfortable booths, and quick service. Kids get books as soon as they sit down. *1306 12th St., Hood River (541) 308-0005*
- **Good River Café :** Chef Barry adds his special touch to your Pacific Northwest dining experience. Meals to write home about. *2nd and Main, Mosier, (541) 478-0111*
- **Joe's El Rio:** Good Mexican/American food, especially the fajitas. *193 Hwy. 14, Stevenson, (509) 427-4479*
- **The Lyle Hotel:** The new owners, who have 3 kids of their own, welcome families with a rich mac'n'cheese. Toys in the lobby. *100*

Seventh St., Lyle, (800) 447-6310, www.lylehotel.com
- **The Mesquitery:** Come hungry for barbequed ribs, chicken or steaks. *1219 12th St., Hood River, (541) 386-2002*
- **Nora's Fish House:** Kids love the clam chowder and fish and chips and the daring child may even try the clams and mussels. *110 Fifth St., Hood River, (541) 387-4000, www.norasfishhouse.com*
- **Pietro's Pizza:** This popular family-eating pizza place has lots of space and a huge game room geared for older kids. *107 2nd St., Hood River, (541) 386-1606*
- **Santacroces' Italian Restaurant:** Some say this Italian restaurant serves the best New York style pizza around. Equipped with toys and books. *4780 Hwy. 35, Hood River, (541) 354-2511*
- **Sixth Street Bistro & Loft:** This popular restaurant serves mostly local and organic/ sustainable food, from the free range chicken to the tasty pear salad. *509 6th St., Hood River, (541) 386-5737, www.sixthstreetbistro.com*
- **Solstice Wood Fire Cafe:** Locals call this one of the best kid-friendly restaurants around. Kids can dine on specially cooked pizza and play in the kids corner full of toys and puzzles. *415 W. Steuben St., Bingen (509) 493-4006, www.solsticewoodfirecafe.com*
- **Sushi Okalani:** A favorite, especially for the Tekka (tuna) rolls and seasweed salad. Go early, it can get crowded. *109 1st St., Hood River, (541) 386-7423, www.sushiokalani.com*
- **Trillium Café:** Western style restaurant has an area filled with kid's toys and board games. *207 Oak St., Hood River, (541) 386-1996*
- **Trout Lake Country Inn:** Locals love the $1 taco night. Games for kids. *15 Guler Rd., (509) 395-3667*

Food To Go _____ 206

- **Lampoei's:** This Thai food stand is one of our favorites. Food is made fresh, so be prepared to wait. Located at the Windance parking lot in Hood River. Closed in the winter
- **Mt. Hood Country Store.** Deli food and drive through coffee. Good stop on the way up or down the mountain. *6545 Cooper Spur Rd., Mt. Hood, (541) 352-6024*
- **Mother's Marketplace:** Besides their lovely name, they sell organic produce, soups, and smoothies that you can eat in the store or take out. A vegan store, no dairy or meat. *104 Hwy. 35, Hood River, (541) 387-2202*
- **Panzanella Artisan Bakery & Italian Deli:** Gourmet breads, pizza and sandwiches, including a peanut butter and jelly sandwich that even adults love. *102 5th St., Hood River, (541) 386-2048*

- **South Bank Kitchen:** Chef Lindsay makes everything from scratch. She also sells high-end gourmet goods and has a "Dinner in the Bank" program where families can easily enjoy homecooked meals. *404 Oak St., Hood River, (541) 386-9876, www.southbankkitchen.com*

Outdoor Seating _____ 203

- **Best Western Hood River Inn:** Consider Sunday brunch on their deck overlooking the river. 1108 East Marina Way, *Hood River, (541) 386-2200, www.hoodriverinn.com*
- **Divots Clubhouse:** While you're waiting for your food and gazing at Mt. Hood, your kids can putter away on the golf course. *3605 Brookside Dr., Hood River, (541) 386-7770, www.indiancreekgolf.com*
- **Elliot Glacier Public House:** Formerly a historic theatre, this pub serves comfort food, like chili, hamburgers and homemade root beer. Locals gather on Monday/Tuesday night for $1.50 tacos. Weather permitting, sit outside and enjoy the view of Mt. Hood. *4945 Baseline Dr., Parkdale, (541) 352-1022*
- **Stonehedge Gardens & Bistro:** During the summer, families dine outside in their garden patio. Try their signature portobello mushroom ravioli. *3405 Cascade Ave., Hood River, (541) 386-3940, www.stonehedgegardens.com.*
- **Hood River Taqueria:** A favorite, especially for the horchata and authentic Mexican food. *1210 13th St., Hood River, (541) 387-3300*
- **Three Rivers Grill:** A premier view from their deck and kids can draw on the tables inside or play across the street at the library. *601 Oak St., (541) 386-8883, www.3riversgrill.com*
- **The Viento Burger and Steak Bar :** Tasty $3 kids burger from natural beef and an outdoor patio where children can roam safely. *216 W. Steuben, Bingen, (509) 493-0049*
- **Walking Man Brewery:** Pizza, beer and salad - you can't go wrong. 240 SW First St., Stevenson, (509)-427-5520, www.walkingmanbrewery.com

Playground Restaurants _____ 204

- **Ranch Drive-In :** Popular with toddlers because half of the dining area is a playroom full of toys. The economic diner serves mainly hamburgers, french fries and shakes. Warning: you may have to wrestle your kids out of the playroom to get them to eat. *1950 12th St., Hood River, (541) 386-1155*

Quick Bites_____205

- **Andrew's Pizza & Bakery:** Thin crust pizza, baked goods and a playroom. Consider pizza and a movie at their Hood River Theater. *107 Oak St., Hood River, (541) 386-1448; 310 S.W. Second St., Stevenson (509) 427-8008, www.skylighttheatre.com*
- **Hood River Bagel Company:** More than 18 different types of bagels, including chocolate chip. *13 Oak St., (541) 386-2123*
- **La Casa de Sabor:** Quick Mexican food, perfect for take-out. *230 1st St., Stevenson, (509) 427-5423*
- **Michoacan:** Delicious authentic carnitas. *3405 Odell Hwy., Odell, (541) 354-2900*
- **New York City Sub Shop:** Large sub sandwiches, and special one-of-a-kind peppers. *1020 Wasco St., Hood River, (541) 386-5144, www.newyorksubshop.com*
- **Pizzicato:** Gourmet pizza, huge salads and speedy service. *2910 W. Cascade Ave., Hood River, (541) 387-2055*
- **Spooky's Pizza:** Families love this place for pizza and games. *3320 W. 6th St., The Dalles, (541) 298-1300*
- **Sub Shop 15 .** Good for a quick sandwich. *1411 Prospect Ave., Hood River, (541) 490-3273*
- **Taco Del Mar:** Known for fish tacos and mission style burritos. The kid's menu includes tacos and burritos. *112 Oak St., Hood River, (541) 308-0030, www.tacodelmar.com*

Chapter 18

Need a Place to Stay?

If you need a roof or tent over your head, this list will get you started. Camping with kids is always an adventure. Remember the chocolate and graham crackers for s'mores. Most hotels these days are kid-friendly. To simplify your hotel search, we just listed the ones with swimming pools.

Campgrounds _____ 207

Oregon
- **Ainsworth State Park:** Great access to hiking, Exit 35 off of I-84 westbound, *(503) 695-2301, www.oregonstateparks.org*
- **Lost Lake Resort:** Camping, fishing, swimming and more. Open May-October. *541-386-6366, www.lostlakeresort.org*
- **Deschutes River State Rec. Area:** big grassy area, biking and swimming, *(800)-452-5687, www.oregonstateparks.org*
- **Memaloose:** Exit 73, 11 miles east of Hood River in Mosier, *(800)-452-5687, www.oregonstateparks.org*
- **Mt. Hood National Forest:** For backpacking/camping at Vista Ridge, Tilly Jane or Cloud Cap, *(503) 668-1700, www.fs.fed.us*
- **Tucker Park:** 5 miles south of Hood River on Dee Hwy., access to the cold river, *541-386-4477, www.co.hood-river.or.us*
- **Tollbridge Park:** 17 miles south of Hood River, *(541) 352-5522, www.co.hood-river.or.us*
- **Viento:** Exit 56 off of I-84, 8 miles west of Hood River, popular with windsurfers, *(541) 387-8811, www.oregonstateparks.org*

Camping and canoeing at Takhlakh Lake

Photo by Chris VanTilburg

Washington
- **Beacon Rock State Park:** Great hiking to the Pool of Winds, *(509) 427-8265, www.parks.wa.gov*
- **Columbia Hills State Park (Horsethief):** home of She who Watches, fishing, grassy area. *(509) 767-1159, www.parks.wa.gov*
- **Gifford Pinchot National Forest:** Trout Lake, Wind River, Mt. Adams area, including Takhlakh Lake, a prime canoeing and camping destination. *(509) 395-6002, www.fs.fed.us/gpnf*
- **Maryhill State Park/ Peach Beach:** Popular with the windsurfing crowd, right on the river, *(509) 773-4698, www.parks.wa.gov*
- **Roosevelt/ Rock Creek:** 17 miles east of Maryhill
- **Timberlake Hall Camping:** a few miles inland from Home Valley. 112 Bylin Rd., *(509) 427-CAMP, www.timberlakehallcamping.com*

Vacation Rentals _____ 208

- **Columbia Gorge Vacation Rental:** *(866) 312-2312, www.columbiagorgevacationsrentals.com*
- **Gorge Central Vacation Rentals.** *(541) 386-6109, www.gorgecentral.com*
- **Gorge Rentals.** *(800) 387-4787, www.GorgeRentals.com*

Hotels with Pools _____ 209

- **Best Western Hood River:** 1108 E. Marina Way, Hood River, *541-386-2200, www.hoodriverinn.com*
- **Best Western Cascade Locks:** 735 WaNaPa St., Cascade Locks, *(800) 595-7108, www.bestwestern.com/columbiariverinn*
- **Bonneville Hot Springs Resort & Spa:** 1252 East Cascade Dr., North Bonneville, *866-459-1678, www.bonnevilleresort.com*
- **Comfort Inn:** 351 Lone Pine Dr., The Dalles, *(541) 298-2800, www.comfortinn.com*
- **Skamania Lodge:** 1131 SW Skamania Lodge Way, Stevenson, *800-221-7117, www.skamania.com*
- **Shilo Inn Suites Hotel:** 3223 Bret Clodfelter Way, *The Dalles, 800-222-2244, www.shiloinns.com*
- **Super 8 Motel:** 609 Cherry Heights Rd., The Dalles, *(541) 296-6888, www.super8.com*
- **The Dalles Inn:** 112 W. 2nd St., The Dalles, *(888) 935-2378, www.thedallesinn.com*
- **The Lodge at Government Camp:** *(800)-547-1406, www.thelodgeatgovernmentcamp.com*
- **Timberline Lodge:** *(800)-547-1406, www.timberlinelodge.com*

Appendix A

Local Town Maps

To help you find your way, below are some maps. Not all streets are included, but hopefully enough to give you a sense of the direction.

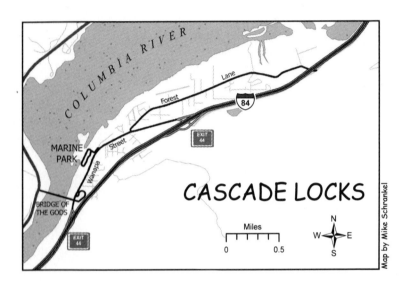

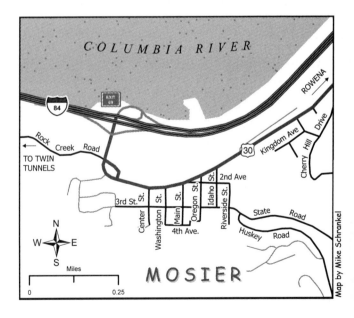

Appendix A - cont.

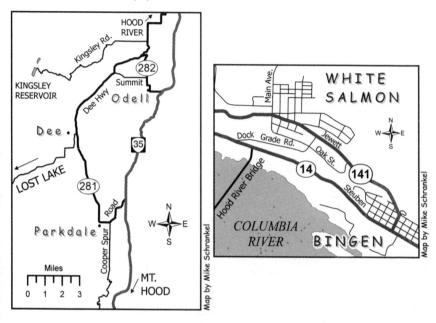

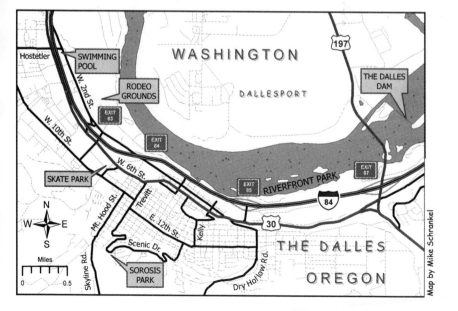

Appendix B

Kidding Around by Area

Index

Notes

Notes